Beyond the Reserve

Beyond the Reserve

*Modern Indigeneity and Cultural Memory
in the Novels of Thomas King*

Rituparna Moharana

BLACK EAGLE BOOKS
Dublin, USA | Bhubaneswar, India

Black Eagle Books
USA address:
7464 Wisdom Lane
Dublin, OH 43016

India address:
E/312, Trident Galaxy, Kalinga Nagar,
Bhubaneswar-751003, Odisha, India

E-mail: info@blackeaglebooks.org
Website: www.blackeaglebooks.org

First International Edition Published by
Black Eagle Books, 2025

BEYOND THE RESERVE
by **Rituparna Moharana**

Copyright © Rituparna Moharana

All rights reserved. No part of this publication may be reproduced, stored in a retrieval system, or transmitted, in any form or by any means, electronic, mechanical, photocopying, recording or otherwise without the prior permission of the publisher.

Cover & Interior Design: Ezy's Publication

ISBN- 978-1-64560-738-0 (Paperback)

Printed in the United States of America

Dedicated to
My grand parents

CONTENTS

Author's Note   09

CHAPTER ONE
The land remembers   13

CHAPTER TWO
Where the Stories Speak Back   17

CHAPTER THREE
Yearning and Belonging to a Lost Home:
A Study of Medicine River   22

CHAPTER FOUR
Roots and Origins of Native American Storytelling:
A Reading of Green Grass, Running Water   32

CHAPTER FIVE
Configurations of Native Cultural Identity
in Truth and Bright Water   84

CHAPTER SIX
The Territory Ahead for Native Studies
and the Works of Thomas King   102

Work Cited   111

Author's Note

This book comprises five chapters that explore how Thomas King's three novels, *Medicine River*, *Green Grass, Running Water*, and *Truth and Bright Water*, depict the pride, resilience, and cultural reclamation of Native American communities. King's narratives foreground the strength of close-knit Indigenous societies, emphasizing unity and collective memory. The severance of these communal ties often results in personal alienation, which characters seek to overcome through reconnection with their roots and cultural traditions.

Chapter One emphasizes that Indigenous peoples are not disappearing, but instead actively shaping their future through the power of storytelling. Their stories challenge colonial myths, reclaim historical narratives, and reaffirm their deep connection to the land. By embracing their culture and identity, they assert their presence and ensure that their voices and histories remain alive, resisting erasure and reclaiming both power and place in the world.

Chapter Two highlights that Thomas King's

storytelling is a form of resistance. By rejecting linear, colonial narratives and embracing Indigenous perspectives, he challenges dominant representations and affirms the ongoing complexity of Native identity. His work not only responds to colonialism but also encourages readers to actively engage with Indigenous stories, recognizing that they are living, evolving, and still being told.

Chapter Three explains that in *Medicine River*, Thomas King blends traditional and modern elements through a storytelling style rich in humor and oral rhythm. By grounding Will's story in a resilient and adaptive community, King challenges conventional ideas about fiction and identity, showing that Indigenous life is dynamic and enduring, not something of the past, but a story still being lived.

Chapter Four describes that King's literary project *Green Grass, Running Water* is one of reclamation, of identity, of narrative authority, and of the land itself. His nuanced, often humorous explorations of cultural hybridity, ecological harmony, and storytelling traditions reveal a vision of Indigenous life that is dynamic, resilient, and deeply rooted in both history and possibility.

Chapter five shows how *Truth and Bright Water* explores the complexities of Indigenous identity, survival, and resistance in a colonial context. Helen's quilt symbolizes both personal and political struggles, highlighting the need to reclaim Native identity through cultural expression and communal participation. The narrative critiques the ongoing effects of colonialism while offering pathways to decolonization through art, satire, and community.

Chapter six reflects the Native oral storytelling traditions through King's fragmented, non-linear narrative style, which resist Western norms of order and causality. This structure critiques colonialism and reclaims Indigenous voice by emphasizing fluidity, multiplicity, and cultural complexity. Through varied characters, objects, and perspectives, King creates a rich, layered form of storytelling that challenges and redefines traditional literary forms.

❑

CHAPTER-I

The Land Remembers

It holds the ancient whispers of those who lived upon it long before the arrival of settlers, before the planting of crops, and before the promises carved into parchment and cloaked in liberty. The land speaks in languages older than ink and empires, its voice shaped by generations of people who respected it, lived in harmony with it, and created a history that was, until recently, all but forgotten. But no one listened. And those who did were silenced.

America, at its inception, was built on the ideal of liberty, a freedom that, in the words of Benjamin Franklin, made the country home. But the nation's birth was also steeped in contradictions, as Thomas Paine, the idealist rebel, reminded us. He stated, "Where liberty is not, there is my country." For Native peoples and Black Americans, liberty was often a distant, unreachable dream, while the reality was one of bondage and erasure. The grand ideals of liberty stood in stark contrast to the grim realities of the American experience, where freedom for some came at the expense of the subjugation of others. For the

Native people, it meant displacement; for the Black man, it meant slavery.

When the first sails appeared on the horizon, English, French, Spanish, Dutch, the land was already spoken for, not in the legalistic sense of ownership, but in a deeper, spiritual sense of belonging. The land had been lived upon, sung to, and understood in ways that settlers could not imagine. Yet, the newcomers brought with them not only flags and Bibles but also diseases that decimated the original stewards of the land. By the mid-1600s, Native populations were decimated, and their communities were irreversibly altered. The land bled quietly as entire cultures were erased from the earth.

The belief in Manifest Destiny, the divine mission to expand the United States across the continent, served as the justification for the violent conquest of Native lands. Treaties were signed with promises that were later broken, and the Indian Removal Act of 1830 forcibly uprooted entire nations, sending them along the Trail of Tears. This brutal act of relocation left scars on the collective memory of Indigenous peoples. By the 20th century, Native Americans found themselves neither fully gone nor fully restored. Reservations became prisons where culture was outlawed and identity suppressed. But through it all, the heartbeat of the land persisted, a quiet defiance against the forces of erasure.

Yet, despite the efforts to silence them, stories survived. They lived on in the whispers around fire rings, in the quiet prayers of elders, and in the songs passed down through generations. Thomas King, a Cherokee author, recognized the power of storytelling in the face of overwhelming odds. His works, including *Medicine River, Green Grass, Running Water,* and *Truth and Bright Water,* served as maps for navigating an identity fractured by history and contemporary politics. King's storytelling was not loud or combative but instead sly, playful, and deeply insightful. In his novels, King reminded readers that resistance can take many forms, sometimes even in the form of laughter.

In the cities, Native men and women began to return, not to the land, but to themselves. Many had served in wars, fighting for a country that had tried to erase them, only to be forgotten once the fighting ceased. Yet a shift occurred. Activism blossomed in the 1960s and 1970s, with the 1973 protest at Wounded Knee becoming a pivotal moment in the fight for Native American rights. This protest forced the U.S. government to confront the history it had long ignored. Self-determination was no longer something to be given; it was something to be demanded. Native peoples began to assert their voices, reclaiming their identity and their place in the broader narrative of American history.

Today, over 560 Native American tribes are federally recognized. But recognition does not equate to restoration. Many Native communities continue to face poverty, addiction, and violence. However, resilience also persists. Native American Studies, once a niche academic field, has evolved into a movement, a reclamation of voice, vision, and sovereignty. This field is not grounded in nostalgia for a past lost but is a powerful assertion of Native peoples' continuing presence and agency. Across universities, classrooms, and political arenas, Native peoples continue to resist, rebuild, and redefine their place in the world.

This narrative is not one of simple loss but of resistance, a story of survival, reclamation, and recovery. As Thomas King often reminds us, "The truth about stories is, that's all we are." The stories that were once stolen, suppressed, or erased are now returning, speaking back to the world. Native peoples, once forgotten or overlooked, are now telling their stories, asserting their right to define their own place in the world. The land still speaks, and those who have been silenced are finally listening.

In this context, the legacy of Indigenous peoples is not one of fading into oblivion but of continuing to shape their future through stories, stories that challenge the myths imposed by colonial powers and reframe the history of the land. By embracing their history, their culture, and their identity, Native peoples ensure that the land will never forget. Through storytelling, they reclaim their power and their place in the world.

❑

CHAPTER-II

Where the Stories Speak Back

Where the Stories Speak Back explores how Indigenous peoples resist erasure, reclaim their identities, and redefine their place in the world through the enduring power of storytelling. Through the narratives of Thomas King, particularly in *Medicine River, Green Grass, Running Water,* and *Truth and Bright Water,* this study reveals the continued struggle for survival, identity, and sovereignty within Indigenous communities in Canada.

In *Medicine River,* the theme of generational conflict and cultural reclamation is highlighted in the interaction between younger and older Indigenous characters. Floyd, one of the younger men, tells Will, "All of you, old men, are trying to recover the past" (146). His remark encapsulates the tension between preserving cultural memory and forging a path forward. Lionel, another character, ultimately chooses to stay in his community, prioritizing the stories he wants to tell over assimilation into a non-Native world. Will, too, returns to Medicine River, where a shared heritage and collective understanding of marginalization offer him emotional grounding in a multicultural but often exclusionary society.

King critiques idealized representations of Indigenous peoples, even in well-received portrayals such as *Dances with Wolves*. He notes how narratives often position Indigenous characters as relics to be "rescued," even as Canada prides itself on multiculturalism, a policy first introduced in 1971 and codified in the Multiculturalism Act of 1988. Despite its promotion of diversity, equality, and tolerance, King's work questions whether multiculturalism genuinely fosters inclusion or simply masks ongoing hierarchies and exclusions.

In *Medicine River*, the notion of community is deeply explored through Will's relationships, especially with Harlen Bigbear, whose sense of survival extends beyond the personal to the communal. Harlen believes in carrying and sharing others' burdens, offering Will not only friendship but a renewed sense of purpose. Will's romantic development with Louise Heavyman, a Native woman, is subtly encouraged by community figures like Martha Old Crow, reinforcing the idea that belonging is nurtured through emotional and cultural connections.

Despite these connections, Will's integration into the community remains complex. While he shares deep emotional ties to Medicine River and its people, he also remains on the periphery, shaped by past traumas and the inability to fully assimilate. The community, presented as a private world, struggles for survival amidst both internal divisions and external pressures. The lack of interaction between Natives and non-Natives in Medicine River, as Garry Williams observes, suggests a polarization that is both chosen and imposed.

The character of Joe Bigbear represents Indigenous presence in broader society. He exhibits Native traditions to outsiders and mocks Will for his cultural ambivalence, emphasizing the complexities of identity performance. Similarly, Lionel James, an elder, travels the world sharing stories and performing traditional dances, pointing to a growing global curiosity about Indigenous culture. Yet this visibility is often superficial, failing to address the deeper cultural and historical narratives at play.

Margaret Atwood, in her essay "A Double Thomas King," highlights how King's storytelling gives voice and identity to Indigenous peoples, helping them reconnect with their roots while also envisioning a distinct future. *Green Grass, Running Water* and *Medicine River* are grounded in specific geographic and cultural contexts, yet King deliberately avoids tribal or rigid geographical identification, suggesting that cultural identity transcends static definitions.

Marlene Goldman notes that King's storytelling disrupts Western narrative structures, using road trips and nonlinear trajectories to challenge dominant cultural assumptions. Critics such as Margery Fee and Jane Flick describe King's method as promoting "nativism through culture, identification and dwelling," where mythic trickster figures help reshape colonial myths into pathways of cultural healing and resistance.

King further explores the dynamics of cultural identity in *Truth and Bright Water*. Here, characters struggle with historical borders, internalized racism, and the commercialization of Native culture. Monroe Swimmer, a surreal figure and famous Indigenous artist, embodies cultural restoration. He repaints colonial church structures into the landscape, buries repatriated skulls in the river, and hosts a "giveaway" celebration, symbolizing renewal, resistance, and spiritual healing.

The symbolic use of water throughout King's novels, especially the dam in *Green Grass, Running Water* and the river rituals in *Truth and Bright Water*, represents the flow of culture and identity. Water becomes a metaphor for continuity, transformation, and reclamation. Through these acts, King underscores how cultural rituals, mythologies, and storytelling are not relics of the past but vital forces shaping contemporary Indigenous life.

Stuart Hall's theorization of cultural identity helps illuminate King's approach. Hall posits two positions: one sees identity as a stable, shared heritage, while the other views it as fluid, shaped by history and power. King seems to navigate both, affirming collective memory while highlighting individual and evolving cultural experiences. His characters, like Helen, a beautician with aspirations of acting, and Cassie, a globe-trotting figure with a shadowy past, embody this duality, torn between self-expression and cultural grounding.

In festivals such as Indian Days, King

illustrates the vibrancy and resilience of Indigenous cultures. These events, filled with races, rituals, and performances, celebrate community while subtly critiquing the gaze of outsiders, particularly tourists fascinated by romanticized versions of "Indianness." Through characters like Tecumseh and Monroe Swimmer, King captures the joy, contradictions, and resistance embedded in these celebrations.

Ultimately, Thomas King's storytelling is an act of resistance. It rejects linear narratives, challenges colonial representations, and affirms the complexity and persistence of Indigenous identity. In doing so, King not only speaks back to dominant cultural frameworks but invites his readers to listen, and to understand that the stories are still unfolding.

❑

CHAPTER-III

Yearning and Belonging to a Lost Home: A Study of Medicine River

Thomas King, in his novel *Medicine River*, offers a refreshing and nuanced portrayal of contemporary Indigenous identity and community. By resisting reductive stereotypes and highlighting the cultural richness of Native communities, King engages in a postcolonial literary act of reclamation, asserting Indigenous presence, resilience, and humor. The central themes of the novel, community, self-discovery, and humor, reveal a deep commitment to dismantling colonial narratives and replacing them with representations rooted in Indigenous cultural values.

King aligns himself with Native writers such as D'Arcy McNickle, N. Scott Momaday, Leslie Silko, and Louise Erdrich, all of whom explore the deeper, often invisible, strengths of Indigenous cultures. Rather than focusing solely on poverty or addiction, they emphasize ceremony, storytelling, and humor. King's own narrative approach reflects this philosophy, favoring character-driven stories infused with community dynamics and everyday resilience.

At the heart of *Medicine River* is Will, a photographer who returns to the fictional town of Medicine River, Alberta, and gradually reconnects with his Indigenous heritage. Will's journey is marked by his interactions with Harlen Bigbear, a charismatic and meddling community figure who embodies both traditional values and contemporary strategies of community building. Through Harlen's encouragement, Will becomes enmeshed in a web of familial and communal relationships that challenge his sense of isolation and his previous detachment from his cultural roots.

King deliberately juxtaposes the realities of modern Native life with the stereotypical images perpetuated by mainstream non-Native narratives. By doing so, he offers an image of a Native community that is dynamic, self-aware, and capable of forward movement. His characters are not passive victims but active participants in their cultural survival. White characters in the novel, when present, often serve as foils, fascinated by or ignorant of the complexities of Indigenous life, thereby highlighting the multidimensionality of Native identity.

The invocation of the phrase "all my relations" underscores a cultural ethos rooted in interconnectedness. This principle of relationality permeates the novel and informs its ethical framework. Will's gradual realization of his belonging is not merely a personal journey but a collective reconnection, facilitated by relationships with characters such as Louise Heavyman and her daughter, South Wing.

Humor serves as both a narrative device and a cultural marker. King's use of irony, wit, and gentle satire demystifies preconceived notions about Indigenous peoples while affirming the vitality of Indigenous worldviews. Harlen's comically intrusive nature and his efforts to re-socialize Will reflect a deeper cultural imperative to maintain community cohesion and intergenerational support.

The novel also addresses serious issues, including domestic violence, suicide, and the legacy of colonial laws such as the Indian Act. Will's mixed heritage and his status under Canadian law complicate his claim to Indigeneity, yet King frames this complexity as intrinsic to the contemporary Native experience. Scenes involving the Department of Indian Affairs (DIA) illustrate the bureaucratic obstacles that Native people face, while emphasizing their resilience and determination to assert identity regardless of official recognition.

Basketball, a recurring motif in the novel, symbolizes community solidarity and resilience. It becomes a metaphor for the collective effort required to preserve culture and identity. Through basketball games, practices, and shared memories, King illustrates how cultural traditions can be reimagined in modern forms.

The natural world plays an integral role in shaping the narrative's spiritual and cultural dimensions. Descriptions of landscapes like Ninastiko (Chief Mountain) ground the story in place and tradition.

Harlen's connection to the land and his teachings about nature echo Indigenous cosmologies that see the Earth as a living, sustaining presence.

Ultimately, *Medicine River* is a story of return, not just of a man to a town, but of a people to themselves. Through Will's journey, King emphasizes that cultural identity is not static or essentialist but a living, evolving relationship with community, land, and story. Harlen, as the symbolic spider weaving the community web, represents the ongoing effort to repair and maintain these bonds. His actions, however unconventional, are deeply rooted in traditional values of kinship, responsibility, and humor.

In constructing a literary space that honors Indigenous ways of being while engaging critically with contemporary realities, King invites readers to reconsider what it means to belong, not just to a place, but to a people, a history, and a shared future.

Louise Owens aptly observes, "The narration of central stories for Native Americans... is the construction of a reality that begins, always, with the earth." In *Medicine River*, Thomas King constructs just such a reality, a cultural, spiritual, and geographic return to Indigenous identity, anchored in the land and interwoven with story. Medicine River is not merely a town; it is the pulse of belonging, and its surrounding mountains, especially Chief Mountain, act as geographical and emotional anchors. As Harlen Bigbear tells Will, "When we can see the mountain, we know we're home." This single line encapsulates the deep-rooted connection between land and identity, revealing that for many Indigenous peoples, home is defined not by ownership but by presence, memory, and shared heritage.

Despite Will's extended stay in Toronto, his return to Medicine River marks more than a geographical shift, it is a re-rooting of identity. His life in the city was characterized by disconnection and quiet loneliness, a feeling sharpened by his mixed heritage and the absence of a clear community. But back in Medicine River, Will steps into an extended kinship network, informal, complex, yet vital. It is a place where Indigenous relationships extend beyond bloodlines to embrace chosen family, community, and cultural continuity.

One of the clearest representations of this chosen family is Will's evolving relationship with Louise Heavyman and her daughter, Wilma, nicknamed "South Wing." Although not biologically related, Will gradually assumes the role of a father figure, mirroring the responsibilities his own absentee father never fulfilled. His symbolic act of claiming the baby in the hospital ("That one") is both humorous and profound, showing how Indigenous fatherhood and kinship are not dictated by legalities but by presence and responsibility. Will's naming of the child, "South Wing," albeit accidental, is adopted with warmth, blurring the line between joke and tradition, and affirming Will's deeper desire to belong.

The novel continually interrogates what it means to be Indigenous in a modern world. Will's mother, having married a white man, lost her legal status under Canadian law, a policy that once denied women and their children the right to property, residence, and identity within the reserve. The displacement of women like Rose is not just physical; it is cultural. Through Will's narrative, King critiques these colonial structures and calls attention to the lived realities of Canadian Indigenous peoples, realities not always shared with or understood by American Indians or the broader white Canadian population.

The community of Medicine River, and particularly the Friendship Centre and basketball team, provide a space of cultural affirmation and empowerment. Harlen Bigbear's insistence on Will joining the basketball team is not about athletic ability; it is about community engagement. In King's world, sport becomes a metaphor for cooperation, identity-building, and pride. Will's gradual integration into the team mirrors his re-entry into the communal life of Medicine River. The boys admire and look up to him, not just for his presence on the court, but for his reliability, care, and quiet leadership.

At the heart of *Medicine River* is King's deep appreciation for the oral tradition. Through Harlen's ceaseless storytelling and gentle meddling, the community's narrative fabric is continually rewoven. Harlen embodies the role of a modern-day Trickster, not the mythic Coyote, but a real-life version who encourages change through humor, contradiction, and compassionate chaos. He does not impose truth but fosters understanding through story. As Paula Gunn Allen observes, the tribal concept of the sacred hoop, the circle of life and community, is present here. King's narrative style mimics the structure of oral storytelling: nonlinear, associative, and circular, with meaning built through repetition, gesture, and omission.

Will's journey is shaped as much by his absence of history as by the stories he begins to create. His father is a spectral presence, never seen, always imagined. In trying to invent a history for his absent father, Will constructs elaborate narratives, an engineer at Petro-Canada, a globe-trotting humanitarian, all to fill the void left by abandonment. These inventions are less about deception and more about need. As Percy Walton writes, "Will needs a past to forge his identity." This act of storytelling, even when fictional, mirrors the larger cultural practice of narrative-making in Indigenous traditions. Will's internal reconstruction parallels the external community-building he participates in.

Moreover, King's novel refuses to portray Indigenous life as static or romanticized. Characters like Lionel James, who travels the world performing "Indianness" for curious white audiences, expose the commodification of Indigenous identity. Lionel's stories are not false, but they are shaped for consumption, stripped of complexity and reduced to spectacle. This tension, between authentic self-expression and externally imposed roles, runs throughout the novel, challenging the reader to rethink what it means to represent Indigenous culture in a colonial context.

As Will's role in the community deepens, photographing families, caring for Louise and South Wing, attending basketball games, he sheds the isolating identity of the "urban Indian" and becomes part of something larger. The climactic photography session, where nearly a hundred people gather for "immediate family" pictures, humorously and poignantly reframes family not as nuclear but as communal. "Oh," says Harlen, "then we're only talking about fifty people or so." This moment encapsulates the novel's core message: that identity, family, and belonging are not about biology or paperwork, they are about relationship, care, and shared stories.

Ultimately, *Medicine River* offers a nuanced exploration of what it means to be Indigenous in a postcolonial world. Through Will's quiet transformation, King presents a hopeful vision grounded in land, language, and love. The novel affirms that home is not just a place, it is a story continuously told, remembered, and shared.

In *Medicine River*, photography becomes a symbolic gesture toward the construction of community and the reassertion of familial ties. A pivotal moment arrives when Will captures a family portrait by the river, a moment Harlen Bigbear describes as more than a picture, it's a visual affirmation of kinship and belonging. Harlen recounts the complex familial web of Joyce Blue Horn, noting her eleven children, including twins and prominent daughters, emphasizing that family, for the community, extends well beyond the nuclear structure. As Harlen puts it with a characteristic blend of humor and truth: "The photo special is for immediate family," revealing just how expansive "immediate" can be on the reserve.

King utilizes humor to gently dismantle stereotypes about Indigenous peoples, revealing the diverse and dynamic lives within the community. Characters like Lionel James, whose life stories oscillate between athletic prowess and tragic missteps, challenge monolithic representations of Indigenous elders. The community may not fully know Lionel, but they respect him. Through multiple perspectives, Harlen's, Bertha's, and others, King illustrates the richness and contradictions that define human identity, resisting simple categorization.

Central to King's narrative approach is his deep engagement with orature, the oral traditions of storytelling that sustain Indigenous cultures. While King does not speak Cherokee, his prose resonates with the rhythm, cadence, and musicality of oral narration. This "Pan-Indian rhythm" infuses the text, making the written word feel spoken, intimate, and alive.

King's narrative is not linear. Instead, it unfolds in episodes, each story self-contained yet interconnected, mirroring the structure of oral storytelling cycles. This composite novel form, also employed by writers like Louise Erdrich, emphasizes continuity through community, voice, and memory rather than traditional plot development.

The novel's trickster figure, Harlen Bigbear, embodies a central archetype in Native storytelling, playful, manipulative, and wise. Harlen orchestrates events in Will's life with both cunning and care. Through him, King injects humor and subversion into the narrative, challenging colonial norms and expectations. Harlen's warmth and wit act as a guide for Will, and by extension, the reader, into the layered life of the community.

King's landscapes are as evocative as his characters. His descriptions of the prairie, the mountains, and the wind-swept skies reflect a deep spiritual and aesthetic connection to the land. This is not mere setting, it is identity, heritage, and presence.

King's own biography parallels many aspects of *Medicine River*. Like Will, he has worked as a photojournalist and spent significant time in Indigenous communities in Alberta. The absent father figure in the novel reflects King's personal history, including a late-life discovery that his own father, presumed dead, had lived on to form new families. This personal thread weaves into the fictional world, giving emotional weight to Will's complex understanding of heritage.

Moreover, King's broader experience, his work with Native studies, his connection to the Blackfoot community, and his awareness of cross-border Indigenous realities, enrich the authenticity of his writing. His prose emerges not only from research and imagination but from lived experience.

In *Medicine River*, Thomas King marries the traditional and the contemporary, the personal and the communal. His narrative style, infused with humor, humility, and oral rhythm, challenges readers to reconsider the boundaries of fiction, family, and identity. By rooting Will's story in a community that persists and adapts, King affirms that Indigenous life is not a relic of the past, but a vibrant, ongoing story.

CHAPTER-IV

Roots and Origins of Native American Storytelling: A Reading of Green Grass, Running Water

The image of the Indian in Canadian literature has long been shaped by ideological forces of nationalism and romanticism. White characters, in identifying with Indigenous peoples, often draw upon a dual desire: a nationalistic attachment to the land and a romantic idealization of the "primitive" purity of Indigenous life. This depiction, grounded in mythologized pasts and heroic archetypes, grants white characters symbolic ownership of land and literature, while allowing for a nostalgic meditation on the contrast between the natural world and encroaching technological modernity. Such portrayals, however, freeze Indigenous culture in a temporal stasis, positioning it as anachronistic and vulnerable to the so-called progress of Western civilization.

Colonialism has not only constructed reductive stereotypes but has institutionalized control over Indigenous communities through legal, social, and spatial mechanisms. The creation of reserves in 1800s Canada segregated Indigenous populations and isolated them from broader networks. Janice Acoose points out that this isolation fostered a perception among Indigenous peoples that their socio-economic challenges were internal failings, rather than consequences of colonial structures. This perception allowed colonial authorities to suppress Indigenous autonomy and silence Indigenous voices, except when they aligned with colonial expectations.

Autonomy is a central concept in Blackfoot culture, as noted by anthropologist Alice B. Kehoe. This autonomy is deeply relational, rooted not in individualism but in a communal context, as Paula Gunn Allen and Elleke Boehmer have also observed. This distinction underscores a fundamental difference between Western and Indigenous epistemologies: where Western culture views identity and gender as fixed, Indigenous perspectives see them as fluid and interconnected with community.

Thomas King's *Green Grass, Running Water* interrogates these dynamics through a layered narrative that intertwines myth, contemporary life, and satire. The novel explores the dissonance between stereotypical "Indians" and the lived realities of modern Indigenous people. It also probes the tension between technological society and the natural world, and the potential of storytelling as a subversive method to preserve and transmit Indigenous culture.

King's characters navigate a world where their identities are continuously reshaped by external assumptions. The protagonist, Lionel Red Dog, must confront his own personal failures while participating in a broader cultural renewal orchestrated by four mysterious elders. These elders, who challenge linear narrative conventions, act in concert with Coyote and offer a counter-narrative to colonial histories. Their insistence on revisiting stories and relationships highlights the Indigenous value of "caring for your relationships", a concept that blends personal responsibility with communal harmony.

King's writing also addresses the struggle over naming and self-identification. Whether "Native," "Indian," "First Nations," or "Aboriginal," the terminology reflects deeper battles over representation, agency, and cultural self-definition. By reclaiming the right to name and narrate, King destabilizes colonial semiotics and affirms the vitality of Indigenous traditions.

The novel resists the static, essentialist "imaginary Indian" trope and instead presents Indigenous characters who are dynamic, self-aware, and capable of transforming their realities. Through strategies such as humor, mythic storytelling, and cultural braiding, King's characters reclaim space within a dominant culture that seeks to assimilate and erase them.

This discourse resonates with James Tully's critique of multicultural constitutionalism. Tully argues that modern societies, though nominally multicultural, often misunderstand cultural diversity through the "billiard ball" model, viewing cultures as isolated, static, and homogenous. Such assumptions hinder genuine recognition and accommodation of cultural difference. True justice, Tully asserts, requires moving beyond nationalistic frameworks and embracing pluralistic modes of governance that honor Indigenous autonomy without forcing conformity to the nation-state model.

In sum, *Green Grass, Running Water* is not merely a novel about contemporary Indigenous life; it is a powerful intervention in ongoing debates about identity, autonomy, and the politics of representation. By reimagining storytelling as a site of resistance and regeneration, King offers a model for Indigenous cultural resurgence in the face of historical and ongoing colonialism.

In Thomas King's *Green Grass, Running Water*, the primary source of strength for Indigenous men and women struggling to affirm their identities lies in community, particularly the community centered on the reserve. While the novel plays with layers of satire, myth, and magical realism, it also addresses serious political concerns, especially the usurpation of Indigenous rights to land. King's characters hear the Canadian national anthem not as a patriotic hymn, but as a symbol of colonization: "Hosanna da, our home in the land of the natives" (299). Canada's multicultural landscape, where Black and white, Indigenous and settler, men and women coexist, raises a central question: how do we reconcile our differences in a way that is just?

King begins his answer with Genesis. His version features Coyote, a trickster figure from Indigenous oral tradition, present at the time of creation, disrupting the ordered universe with chaotic energy. One of Coyote's dreams gains autonomy and delusions of grandeur, declaring, "I don't want to be a little god. I want to be a big god!" (3). This dream-god, loud and arrogant, introduces an alternative theology and re-centers creation around Indigenous wit and worldview. King's reimagining is not simply parody; it is a form of decolonial resistance. Through Coyote and other trickster characters, King exposes the cultural assumptions embedded in dominant narratives.

Biblical reinterpretations are central to this deconstruction. The novel offers a revisionist account of the Garden of Eden, where "First Woman" falls from the sky and builds a life with Ahdamn, until God arrives, feigning ignorance of their existence. By retelling these foundational stories through Indigenous perspectives, King offers not only cultural critique but a profound act of reclamation.

This revisionist strategy is not merely narrative play; it is political. The Western canon, particularly biblical and colonial myths, has long justified imperial domination. As King's narrator declares, the purpose of retelling these stories is "to deconstruct those nations and processes that rationalized the imposition of the imperial word on the rest of the world" (Cox 231). In other words, storytelling becomes a method of cultural survival and resistance.

At the heart of *Green Grass, Running Water* is Lionel Red Dog, a full-blooded Blackfoot man who has been assimilated into settler society. Living in the fictional town of Blossom, Alberta, Lionel sells electronics and dreams of returning to university like his uncle Eli. Eli, a once-assimilated academic, retreats from the settler world to live in a cabin beneath the Grand Baleen Dam, a literal and symbolic barrier between Indigenous life and colonial development. Like Will in *Medicine River*, Lionel embodies the tension between tradition and assimilation. However, unlike Will, Lionel's internal conflict is more pronounced, and his narrative arc is explicitly shaped by spiritual intervention.

Lionel's identity crisis unfolds alongside an intervention by four mythic figures, Lone Ranger, Ishmael, Robinson Crusoe, and Hawkeye, who claim they are "fixing the world" (123). These ancient Indians, like Harlen Bigbear in *Medicine River*, act as omnipresent guides, nudging Lionel toward a fuller acceptance of his heritage. After a series of humorous but transformative encounters, Lionel experiences a symbolic rebirth. Disgusted with his job and his life, he decides to return to university, a move symbolizing his re-engagement with Indigenous values and intellectual sovereignty.

Water imagery permeates this transformation. The recurring presence of puddles and downpours, culminating in the breaking of the dam, represents both destruction and cleansing. Coyote and the four old Indians conjure the flood as a spiritual act, washing away the barriers between Lionel and his cultural self. The flood also literalizes the novel's critique of colonial infrastructure and its disregard for Indigenous land.

A particularly potent image is "The Map", a wall

of televisions arranged to resemble North America, through which Bill Bursum plays westerns. The Map symbolizes Western dominance, not only over land but over narrative itself. Lionel, mesmerized by John Wayne films, internalizes a settler mythos where cowboys are heroes and Indigenous people are villains. His admiration for Wayne signifies a denial of his Indigeneity. But this myth is destabilized when the four old Indians use their powers to rewrite the film. The Indians win; John Wayne is killed. Lionel, now wearing a fringed leather jacket (a birthday gift resembling the cowboy costume), must choose: will he continue to idolize colonial heroes, or will he embrace the spiritual and cultural guidance of his ancestors?

King uses Lionel's jacket, the film, and the Map to symbolize the internalized colonization that many Indigenous people navigate. The leather jacket, initially admired for its Western flair, eventually resembles the bullet-riddled costume of the fallen John Wayne. The gift becomes both a critique of settler culture and a test of Lionel's allegiance. Will he, like the fictional George Morningstar, disrespect sacred traditions for personal gain? Or will he follow Eli and the four old Indians toward a more rooted existence?

The novel's climax reaffirms King's vision of spiritual and cultural renewal. Lionel participates in the Sun Dance, standing between Eli and George to protect the sanctity of the ceremony. The Sun Dance becomes the metaphorical and literal center of community life, a place where the divided self might begin to heal.

Even the novel's romantic subplot, Lionel and Charlie's rivalry for Alberta, mirrors this cultural tension. Both men are ashamed of their Indigeneity; both look to Alberta for validation. Alberta's decision to spend the weekend with Lionel suggests a preference for humility and community over corporate assimilation. The destruction of the dam leaves both men jobless but also frees them to rediscover their cultural roots. The final message is subtle yet clear: liberation does not lie in the adoption of settler norms, but in the revitalization of Indigenous ways of being.

In *Green Grass, Running Water*, Thomas King offers no easy answers. Instead, he suggests that the reconciliation of identity requires both story and ceremony. It requires the interruption of colonial myths and the reaffirmation of Indigenous knowledge systems. Through Coyote's mischief and Lionel's journey, King reorients the reader toward a different genesis, one where tricksters, not gods, shape the world, and where healing begins with laughter, land, and story.

In *Green Grass, Running Water*, King challenges the conventional notion of "home" by refusing to situate Native identity exclusively within the boundaries of a reserve. The novel presents an ongoing, dynamic relationship between Native characters and the broader world, reflected in characters like Charlie, who, having left the Blackfoot reserve for California, later returns. This refusal to conform to the "reservation narrative" often found in literature, where Native characters are depicted as either returning to the reserve in despair or being destroyed by the city, pushes back against these reductionist portrayals. As King notes in an interview, many Indigenous people live fluid, cyclical lives, moving between spaces without being confined to any one identity or place.

While characters like Lionel and Charlie, for instance, do not engage directly in overt conflict with colonial structures, *Green Grass, Running Water* adopts a more subversive approach to resistance. The character of Bursum, for example, claims to have lived with Indians for his entire life, yet he fails to recognize the distance and alienation inherent in his attitude. His attempts to position himself as a part of the Native community, even while maintaining an othering stance, highlight the systemic misunderstandings and assumptions held by outsiders.

A key theme in King's work is the interplay between remembering the past and living in the present. Alberta's reaction to her mother Ada's handling of damaged Sun Dance regalia speaks volumes about the pragmatic, survivalist mindset that many Indigenous people adopt in the face of trauma. Ada's refusal to dwell on the past in favor of fixing what can be repaired highlights a resilient, forward-thinking attitude that suggests the past need not define the future. This pragmatic approach to memory and trauma reflects a refusal to be imprisoned by colonial narratives of victimhood, instead offering a vision of Indigenous survival and transformation.

In terms of gender, *Green Grass, Running Water* presents a complex picture of Indigenous women negotiating personal autonomy in a world shaped by colonialism and patriarchy. Alberta, in particular, represents a powerful narrative of resistance to traditional roles. Her decision to leave her controlling husband Bob, a man who expects her to sacrifice her academic career and dreams for a conventional, heteronormative marriage, illustrates a rejection of imposed gender expectations. Alberta's eventual decision to have a child on her own, defining her own sense of family, further subverts colonial and patriarchal narratives about women's roles within society.

King's storytelling style in *Green Grass, Running Water* draws heavily from oral tradition, reflecting the way in which Indigenous stories are passed down and continuously reshaped. The novel's structure, with its fractured and overlapping narratives, mirrors the fluidity of oral storytelling, where time and space are not fixed but instead bend to the needs of the storyteller. King even incorporates Cherokee syllabics into the text, signaling a deep connection to Indigenous linguistic traditions while also emphasizing the importance of translation, interpretation, and adaptation in the telling of stories.

The interplay of myth and history in the novel becomes a site of resistance. King's characters, particularly the four escaped mental patients who play a pivotal role in the narrative, function as trickster figures, much like Coyote, who subvert the Western linear narrative of time and the "official" historical record. Through humor and parody, King critiques the way in which Western culture insists on categorizing and confining knowledge, while also suggesting that Indigenous worldviews, shaped by fluid, interconnected, and cyclical understandings of time, offer a more holistic and flexible approach to knowledge and survival.

The novel's postmodern sensibility is characterized by its playful irreverence toward canonical Western narratives. King's hybridization of the Bible with Western pop culture, most notably through the figures of Lone Ranger, Robinson Crusoe, and Ishmael, creates a parody that destabilizes the authority of both mythological and historical narratives. These characters, stripped of their traditional heroic roles, are transformed into Indigenous trickster figures, capable of navigating and reshaping the world around them. In doing so, King challenges the entrenched power structures that have historically marginalized Indigenous voices.

King's *Green Grass, Running Water* further subverts these dominant narratives by presenting an alternative cosmology. The novel suggests that the very foundations of Western thought, including the biblical creation story, can be reimagined through an Indigenous lens. Through the interactions of Coyote with God and other figures, King proposes a playful yet profound critique of the Eurocentric worldview that seeks to impose order on chaos and define meaning through rigid systems of power and control.

Through *Green Grass, Running Water*, Thomas King demonstrates that Native literature is not only a means of preserving culture but also a tool for actively reimagining history and identity. The novel resists a fixed sense of "home" and instead embraces a fluid, dynamic understanding of Indigenous life. It critiques the imposition of Western norms and exposes the limitations of colonial thought by offering an Indigenous perspective that is both subversive and transformative. King's narrative strategy, steeped in humor, mythology, and parody, encourages readers to reconsider their assumptions about history, culture, and identity, ultimately presenting a more complex, multifaceted view of the Native experience. In doing so, *Green Grass, Running Water* stands as a testament to the resilience and creativity of Indigenous people, offering a narrative that defies easy categorization and invites readers to participate in the ongoing process of decolonization.

In *Green Grass, Running Water*, Thomas King uses the trickster figure, Coyote, to present an alternative vision of the world. This aligns with the Native American worldview, where the emphasis is on balance and harmony rather than the binary dichotomy of good and evil found in Judeo-Christian teachings. As King explains, the trickster figure, a cheater or deceiver, plays a crucial role in challenging the established order and presenting a new way of understanding the world. Coyote's antics disrupt conventional narratives and create a space for Native American cosmology, where the world is in constant flux, and all things are interconnected. In this context, Coyote's role is not only to play tricks but also to restore balance to a world that has been altered by colonization.

The novel is structured into four parts, each guided by repeated motifs that reveal the underlying principles of Native American storytelling. These motifs include a sacred color for the Cherokee, a sub-narrative controlled by the four old Indians, the feminine origins of each of the ancient characters, and a Western canon narrative, which ties postcolonial themes into the relationship between the central white character and the secondary indigenous one. Coyote's presence is woven throughout each part, appearing as a guiding figure who facilitates the characters' journeys toward rediscovering their Native heritage and identity.

Coyote's intervention is essential for the four old Indians, who work together to "fix the world." The flood that concludes the novel, resulting from the breaking of a dam on Blackfoot land, symbolizes the intrusion of white settler colonialism. The dam, built as a symbol of white technological superiority, is ultimately sabotaged by Coyote, who uses the very technology of the colonizers against them. This act of environmental trickery represents a powerful metaphor for the way in which indigenous cultures have been forced to adapt, resist, and reclaim their power in a world that continually seeks to undermine them.

The destruction of the dam, as well as the subsequent flooding, leads to a symbolic return home for the novel's characters. In the aftermath of the flood, Lionel Red Dog, who has struggled with his identity throughout the story, decides to rebuild his grandmother's cabin, the structure that once served as a symbol of family and heritage. This rebuilding is not merely physical; it is a symbolic act of reclaiming his place within the community and embracing his Blackfoot identity. By reconnecting with his roots and his people, Lionel finds his sense of belonging.

Humor plays a crucial role in King's novel, particularly in the trickster's antics. Coyote's humorous interventions invite readers to rethink the seriousness with which Western narratives are often regarded. In Native American oral tradition, humor is not just a tool for entertainment; it is a means of teaching important lessons about the world and human nature. Through Coyote's pranks, King encourages readers to challenge dominant cultural narratives and embrace a more fluid, interconnected understanding of reality.

At the heart of *Green Grass, Running Water* is the idea of storytelling as a tool for healing and reclaiming identity. In Native American cultures, stories are not merely for entertainment; they carry profound responsibilities, shaping individuals' understanding of who they are and where they come from. The novel underscores the importance of storytelling in maintaining and strengthening tribal identity. Through the repetition of creation stories, King reinforces the idea that the past, present, and future are interconnected, and that returning to one's origins is an essential step in healing from the trauma of colonialism.

Lionel's journey throughout the novel reflects the process of rediscovering one's identity. Initially alienated from his culture, Lionel is unsure of who he is or where he belongs. He yearns to be like John Wayne, the epitome of the heroic, white, Western figure. However, as the story unfolds, Lionel learns that his true identity is rooted in his Native heritage. With the help of his aunt Norma and the intervention of the four old Indians, Lionel begins to reconnect with his roots and embrace his Blackfoot identity. His journey of self-discovery culminates in his decision to take part in the Sun Dance, a sacred ceremony that signifies his return to the community and his commitment to preserving his tribal traditions.

The novel also emphasizes the role of women in Native American societies, particularly in the preservation and transmission of cultural values. The first woman and her sister characters embody the respect for women's wisdom, strength, and autonomy within Native cultures. These women work to maintain relationships and harmony within their communities, counteracting the patriarchal structures imposed by Western colonialism. Unlike the divisive actions of Eve in the Biblical creation story, the women in *Green Grass, Running Water* seek to foster unity and understanding, reflecting the Native American value of interconnectedness.

In the end, *Green Grass, Running Water* is a novel about reclaiming identity, community, and the power of storytelling. By incorporating traditional Native American values and techniques, King offers a critique of Western colonial narratives and proposes an alternative vision of the world, one that values balance, harmony, and respect for all living beings. Through Coyote's tricks, the four old Indians' efforts to "fix the world," and Lionel's journey toward self-acceptance, the novel underscores the importance of returning to one's roots and reaffirming one's place in the community. The process of reclaiming identity is not linear but cyclical, rooted in the telling of stories and the restoration of relationships that have been fractured by colonization.

Thomas King's *Green Grass, Running Water* offers a profound examination of Native American identity and culture through the lens of postcolonial narratives, blending humor, myth, and modern realities. At the heart of this exploration is the trickster figure, embodied by Coyote, who acts as a conduit for indigenous cosmology and offers an alternative vision of the world. This trickster challenges the conventional dichotomy of good versus evil found in Western thought, replacing it with a focus on balance, harmony, and interconnectedness, key values in Native American worldviews.

King's novel is structured around four primary parts, each emphasizing different elements of Native culture and mythology. These parts include a sacred color for the Cherokee, sub-narratives controlled by the four old Indians, and the feminine origins of each of the ancient Indian deities. The narrative unfolds through a postcolonial framework, exploring the relationship between white and indigenous characters and the way colonialism has shaped their identities. The opening and closing chapters feature Coyote as the narrator, reinforcing the trickster's role as both a disruptive and transformative force within the story.

The novel's central figure, Lionel Red Dog, undergoes a significant journey toward rediscovering his Native identity, which mirrors the broader theme of the search for roots within indigenous communities. Lionel's internal conflict, symbolized by his fascination with the heroic figure of John Wayne, reflects the alienation many indigenous people experience in a world dominated by white narratives and values. Through his interactions with Coyote and the four old Indians, Lionel's return to his cultural heritage becomes a process of self-discovery, where the reconnection with his tribe is not merely geographical but ideological, as he embraces the communal and storytelling traditions that bind him to his ancestors.

The role of women in *Green Grass, Running Water* is also pivotal. In King's portrayal, women are not divisive figures but caretakers of relationships, responsible for maintaining the strength and cohesion of their communities. This is in direct contrast to the patriarchal, individualistic values of Western Christianity. The female characters in the novel, particularly the First Woman, reflect the Native tradition of honoring women for their wisdom, strength, and autonomy. These characters work to resist colonial structures without engaging in a direct confrontation with Western values. Instead, their resistance lies in their ability to nurture relationships and uphold the traditions that sustain Native communities.

The storytelling tradition is another essential

component of King's novel. Indigenous narratives, which often circle back to their beginning, emphasize the process of returning home and reconnecting with one's roots. The function of storytelling in Native American cultures is not only to entertain but to teach and heal, reinforcing identity and relationships. In *Green Grass, Running Water*, the circular nature of storytelling reflects the ongoing process of cultural reclamation, as Lionel's journey is mirrored in the stories of the four old Indians, who "fix" the world through the act of telling stories. These stories do not simply recount the past but actively participate in the creation and re-creation of identity, as each retelling offers new insights and opportunities for healing.

One of the novel's most significant thematic concerns is the reclamation of Native identity, which Lionel eventually achieves. His journey is shaped by his interactions with his family and community, particularly his aunt Norma, who represents the wisdom of the elders. Her use of storytelling as a means of guiding Lionel back to his roots highlights the inseparable link between personal identity and tribal identity in Native cultures. This journey of self-discovery culminates in Lionel's participation in the Sun Dance ceremony, a moment of cultural reaffirmation that signifies his return to his rightful place within the Blackfoot community.

Humor, too, plays an integral role in the novel. As Vina Deloria, Jr. has noted, humor is a central component of Native American storytelling, often used to unite communities and offer a way of navigating difficult truths. In *Green Grass, Running Water*, the trickster figure of Coyote brings both chaos and clarity, serving as a humorous reminder of the contradictions inherent in both Native and Western worldviews. Through Coyote's antics and the novel's use of satire, King invites readers to question established narratives and reconsider the roles of history, identity, and cultural survival in the face of colonialism.

The novel's resolution, marked by the breaking of the dam and the rebuilding of Lionel's grandmother's cabin, symbolizes the restoration of cultural continuity and the restoration of balance in the world. Just as the ancient stories and creation myths are told again to "fix" the world, Lionel's return to his Native identity represents a broader reclamation of cultural sovereignty. In this way, King's *Green Grass, Running Water* not only recounts the complexities of Native American life in the face of colonialism but also reaffirms the power of storytelling to heal, transform, and restore communities. Through humor, myth, and narrative structure, King creates a space where Native identities are reclaimed, and the process of cultural healing is ongoing, reminding us of the enduring importance of stories in shaping our understanding of the world.

In *Green Grass, Running Water*, Thomas King masterfully integrates Native American storytelling traditions to explore themes of identity, cultural renewal, and resistance to colonial oppression. Central to this exploration is the idea of a 'renewal ceremony' or 'ritual act' that restores tribal identity and reconnects the individual with the community. This theme is embodied through the protagonist, Lionel Red Dog, whose journey of self-discovery mirrors the broader narrative of reclaiming Native identity in the face of historical trauma.

The novel portrays a symbolic homecoming for Lionel through his participation in the Sun Dance, a powerful ritual that signifies his return to his roots. Although Lionel was born on the reserve, his earlier life was marked by a departure from his heritage. His return to the Sun Dance Lodge is a physical and spiritual homecoming that reaffirms his Native identity and reconnects him with his community. This 'renewal ceremony' is not only about reconnecting with the past but also about finding one's place within the community, as the rituals of the Sun Dance offer an opportunity to heal and to reaffirm one's ties to ancestral traditions.

King emphasizes the role of oral tradition in this process of renewal. The protagonists, particularly Lionel, are encouraged to tell their stories to future generations, thus participating in the cyclical nature of oral storytelling. This tradition not only affirms identity but also creates a space for the continuous healing of the community. As Lionel is told by Thought Woman, "In the next few years... you can tell to your children and grandchildren about this" (Green Grass, Running Water 428). This reinforces the notion that the transmission of stories is integral to the maintenance of cultural identity and the healing of the individual and collective spirit.

King also uses humor and mythology to challenge and subvert Western Christian narratives. The characters of Ishmael, Hawkeye, and the Lone Ranger, figures from American literary history and popular culture, serve as a critique of traditional white myths, particularly those related to the control of nature and the idea of the "discovery" of America. The four old Indians, who adopt these white names, challenge the linear, Eurocentric narratives of history by blurring the boundaries between myth, reality, and cultural imagination. In doing so, King critiques the colonial violence embedded in Western epistemologies, particularly the ways in which colonialism has shaped the portrayal of Native peoples.

The four old Indians possess a magical, transformative power that allows them to "fix the world" and alter reality. Their role in the novel is crucial, not only for guiding Lionel back to his heritage but also for helping him reevaluate his position within the intersecting worlds of Native and white cultures. These figures are integral to the novel's larger theme of cultural reclamation, as they embody the power of storytelling and the ability to reshape history through narrative.

King also critiques the impact of colonialism on Native American communities through the lens of popular media and stereotypes. Characters like George Morningstar, who wears a suede jacket in an attempt to connect to an "authentic" Native past, symbolize the disconnection between the realities of Native life and the myths constructed by white society. This image of the "imaginary Indian" reflects the ways in which white culture has distorted and appropriated Native identities for its own purposes. King uses humor and irony to dismantle these stereotypes, urging readers to recognize the difference between the constructed myths and the lived experiences of Native people.

Eli Stands Alone, another key character in the novel, represents a form of resistance to colonial forces. His refusal to leave his family's land in the face of a dam project symbolizes the broader struggle of Native peoples to protect their heritage and cultural practices from external threats. Eli's act of defiance mirrors historical and contemporary acts of resistance, such as the stand of Elijah Harper in Canadian politics. His refusal to allow external forces to dictate the fate of his land and people underscores King's vision of a Native community that is resilient and determined in the face of colonial pressures.

Through these characters and themes, King advocates for the empowerment of Native communities and the reclamation of their cultural heritage. The act of telling one's story is both a personal and collective endeavor, as it reaffirms identity and ensures the survival of cultural traditions. In *Green Grass, Running Water*, King uses the intersection of oral and written traditions to offer a hybrid form of storytelling that acknowledges the complexities of the colonial encounter while affirming the ongoing strength and resilience of Native cultures. The blending of these traditions creates a dynamic space for resistance, renewal, and transformation, suggesting that the future of Native identity lies in the continuous act of storytelling and cultural revitalization.

In *Green Grass, Running Water*, Thomas King intricately weaves Native American mythology into the fabric of Western culture, creating a compelling narrative that blends the sacred with the secular. A key figure in this narrative is Coyote, whose role as an archetype in Native American stories stands in stark contrast to Western narratives, particularly the Christian myth. King admits in an interview with Peter Gzowski that his initial attempt to incorporate Christian mythology felt restrictive. He discovered that in order to fully explore his narrative, he needed the freedom offered by Native oral stories, which allowed him to replace the Genesis creation story with one rooted in Indigenous traditions. In doing so, King seeks to disrupt colonial narratives, blending literary, historical, and oral storytelling traditions to form a dynamic, multi-layered narrative structure.

Coyote's presence is central to this mythic reconstruction. As a trickster and a creator, Coyote not only shapes the universe in the novel but also acts as a symbol of resistance to the dominant cultural narratives. King uses Coyote's disruptive nature to subvert colonial representations, creating a space where Native identities can reclaim their power outside the bounds of Western stereotypes. This is especially evident in the characters and events that emerge in the novel, where the mythic and real collide, and where Native heroes like Lionel Red Dog confront the challenges of living between two worlds.

One of the novel's most poignant symbols is the Sun Dance ceremony, which represents not only cultural renewal but also the reclaiming of identity. Lionel's decision to divide his life into "manageable goals," such as spending more time with his parents and participating in the Sun Dance, signifies his growing connection to his Blackfoot roots. This decision, deeply influenced by the spiritual intervention of the four old Indians, illustrates his return to a community-centered life, echoing the larger narrative of cultural revitalization in the face of colonial disruption.

The Sun Dance, a sacred Indigenous ceremony, is central to the cultural regeneration in the novel. Lionel's journey toward this ceremony marks a transformative moment in his character's evolution. His commitment to accompany his parents to the Sun Dance, a gesture that his father would greatly appreciate, is symbolic of Lionel's attempt to embrace his cultural heritage. This personal evolution mirrors the larger cultural reclamation happening within the Blackfoot community, which resists the pressures of assimilation and colonization. King uses Lionel's growth to suggest that identity is not static but a dynamic, ongoing process shaped by both personal and communal rituals.

The Dead Dog Cafe in the novel exemplifies this tension between cultural authenticity and stereotype. Latisha, the cafe owner, skillfully manipulates the expectations of tourists who seek an "authentic" Native experience. Through her ironic and subversive actions, she deconstructs the myths surrounding Native identity, parodying the stereotypical images of the "savage" Indian. Her engagement with the "tourists" reflects King's critique of the commodification of Native culture, and Latisha's participation in the Sun Dance further underscores the complexity of cultural identity in a modern, hybridized world.

Another major theme in *Green Grass, Running Water* is the assertion of Native autonomy and resistance to colonial powers. The construction of a dam outside the Blackfoot reservation represents a tangible manifestation of the ongoing colonial project, which seeks to control and disrupt Native ways of life. Eli Stands Alone, a key character, embodies this resistance as he refuses to leave his cabin at the base of the dam, symbolizing a stand against the forces of colonialism. His eventual death, as the dam is destroyed, serves as a powerful statement of both sacrifice and triumph, as it illustrates the lengths to which Native individuals must go to protect their land, culture, and way of life.

King also explores the concept of containment, a metaphor for colonial control, through figures such as God and Noah, who represent patriarchal, authoritarian figures intent on limiting and controlling the lives of others. The intersection of these biblical figures with Native figures like Changing Woman, Thought Woman, and Old Woman serves to highlight the tension between the oppressive forces of Western religious and cultural traditions and the transformative power of Native oral traditions.

The dam in the novel is not only a physical barrier but also a symbolic representation of colonial efforts to contain and destroy Native cultures. Its eventual destruction is a triumphant moment in the novel, reflecting the resilience of Indigenous peoples in the face of colonial oppression. Through these symbolic acts of resistance, King challenges the dominant narratives and reclaims the power of storytelling, positioning Native oral traditions as both a form of resistance and a means of cultural survival.

Lionel's personal journey throughout the novel, from his mistakes and missteps to his eventual embrace of his cultural roots, mirrors the larger struggle of Indigenous peoples to navigate the complexities of modern life while maintaining their cultural integrity. King uses Lionel's story to illustrate the difficulties of balancing multiple identities and the tensions that arise when one is caught between two cultures. This struggle is further complicated by the colonizing forces that attempt to define Native identity through a lens of assimilation and stereotype.

Ultimately, *Green Grass, Running Water* is a celebration of the resilience of Native cultures and the power of oral storytelling. King's work asserts that cultural identity is not defined by the colonial narratives imposed upon it but is instead a living, evolving force that can be reclaimed and transformed. By blending Native and Western traditions, King creates a narrative that challenges colonialism while celebrating the strength and vitality of Indigenous cultures.

In Thomas King's novels, particularly *Medicine River* and *Green Grass, Running Water*, relationships serve as a significant lens through which he explores broader cultural dynamics, particularly those between the Native and dominant cultures. King uses various interpersonal relationships to demonstrate how the balance between the center and margin, metaphors for mainstream society and Indigenous communities, can be achieved through mutual understanding and respect. This "spirit of commitment" is a recurring theme in King's work, representing the possibility of harmonious coexistence despite historical tensions.

One of the most poignant examples of this spirit of commitment can be found in the relationship between Louise and Will in *Medicine River*. Their cautious but growing connection symbolizes the potential for mutual respect between the sexes and, by extension, between cultures. Louise expresses her belief that Will will "understand her," emphasizing the importance of understanding and respecting differences. For King, this understanding is a prerequisite for equality, and this theme is explored through the male-female dynamic in the novel. The relationship between Will and Louise is tentative, symbolizing the broader, cautious approach of Indigenous peoples toward the dominant culture, a culture that has historically marginalized and oppressed them. As the center (mainstream culture) and margin (Indigenous cultures) draw closer, there is hope that equality and respect can lead to harmonious coexistence.

King also uses the metaphor of children in mixed marriages as symbols of the future. In *Medicine River*, South Wing, the child of a white father and an

Indigenous mother, is embraced by both sides of the family, demonstrating the potential for cross-cultural understanding and acceptance. This inclusion of mixed-race children reflects King's optimism for the future, as they represent a new generation that may be free from the weight of historical oppression. These children are symbols of both the present and the future King envisions, one where the rigid, colonial definitions of race and identity are dismantled. Through the characters of South Wing and others, King suggests that the future may hold a more fluid and inclusive vision of identity, where the oppression of the past no longer defines the possibilities for future generations.

King also tackles the theme of cultural identity through the lens of land and nature. In *Green Grass, Running Water*, King contrasts the natural world with the encroachment of technology and artificial systems, symbolized by the dam that threatens the Blackfoot community's way of life. For Indigenous peoples, land and nature are not just resources but integral parts of their cultural and spiritual practices. The dam, as an embodiment of technological progress, is portrayed as a force that disrupts the natural flow of life. It is a metaphor for the forces of colonialism and industrialization that seek to control and contain the natural world, and by extension, Indigenous cultures.

The Indigenous resistance to the dam is a powerful act of defiance. For the Blackfoot characters, the natural world represents a fluid, ever-changing cycle of life, growth, and spiritual connection. The dam, on the other hand, represents stagnation and paralysis, an attempt to freeze the world in a state of artificial permanence. The confrontation between these two ideologies, the natural and the technological, symbolizes the clash between Indigenous values and colonial ideologies. As Harley explains to Eli, the dam disrupts the flow of the river, preventing it from nourishing the cottonwoods used in the Sun Dance ceremony. For the Blackfoot, the vitality of the land is intrinsically tied to their cultural practices, and the dam represents a direct threat to their ability to continue these ceremonies, which are vital to their identity.

In this context, King uses the metaphor of the river to represent the ongoing, natural flow of Indigenous culture and identity. Just as the river carries nutrients to the cottonwoods, the practices and traditions of Indigenous peoples flow through generations, providing spiritual nourishment and continuity. The dam, in contrast, is a symbol of colonial efforts to contain, control, and ultimately erase this cultural continuity. The struggle against the dam is not just a physical one but a cultural battle, one that seeks to preserve the fluidity of Indigenous traditions against the rigidity of colonial forces.

Through these themes, King emphasizes the importance of cultural continuity, resistance, and adaptation. His characters' struggles, whether in their personal relationships, their identities as mixed-race individuals, or their fight to preserve their cultural practices, are all part of a broader narrative of resilience and hope. King's work is a testament to the possibility of cultural survival and renewal in the face of ongoing colonial pressures. It is through these acts of resistance, whether through interpersonal relationships or the defense of the land, that King envisions a future where Indigenous peoples can reclaim their stories and continue to thrive in a world that has too often sought to silence them.

In the landscape of Canadian literature, the image of the "Indian" has long served as a malleable symbol for nationalistic and romanticized ideals. Non-Indigenous authors have historically appropriated Native figures to project fantasies of purity, nobility, and closeness to the land, qualities seen as lost in modernity. This symbolic use of the Native as a vessel for white anxieties about technology, nature, and authenticity reinforces colonial narratives. It not only marginalizes Indigenous peoples but erases the complexity of their lives, reducing them to static emblems trapped in a mythical past. Against this backdrop, Thomas King's *Green Grass, Running Water* emerges as a dynamic and subversive response, challenging these distortions through humor, myth, and a fiercely rooted sense of community.

King's work is an act of narrative resistance, a deliberate reweaving of the threads of Indigenous storytelling into the fabric of contemporary literature. In *Green Grass, Running Water*, King introduces Coyote, the quintessential trickster figure, as both a disruptive and creative force. In reimagining the Genesis myth, Coyote not only mocks Western religious authority but also reclaims the act of creation as a communal and fluid process, one not bound by hierarchical divinity but open to Indigenous cosmologies and oral traditions. The irreverent, dreamlike quality of the Coyote narratives destabilizes the linear, patriarchal logic of the Western canon and reinstates the oral storytelling tradition as a site of cultural autonomy.

This narrative approach reflects what Paula Gunn Allen describes as a concept of autonomy that is not individualistic but relational, an identity shaped and sustained through community. King's characters are deeply embedded in their relationships, and their selfhood is constructed through the reciprocity and responsibilities of those relationships. The journey of Lionel Red Dog, the protagonist, becomes emblematic of the tension between assimilation and cultural reclamation. Lionel's initial alienation, from his heritage, his family, and even himself, echoes the larger historical dislocation inflicted by colonial policies such as the reserve system and the Indian Act. His journey is not just one of self-realization, but of communal reconnection and healing.

King portrays Lionel's crisis at age forty as a pivotal moment of reckoning. Through encounters with the four mythical elders, Lone Ranger, Ishmael, Robinson Crusoe, and Hawkeye, Lionel begins to navigate a path between the cultural worlds he inhabits. These elders, who blend historical and literary figures with Indigenous oral tradition, act as guides not just for Lionel, but for readers, illustrating the possibility of new narratives that do not rely on colonial binaries. Their mission to "fix the world" speaks to the transformative power of Indigenous stories, not as static folklore, but as living, breathing forces of resistance and renewal.

Water, as both motif and metaphor, plays a central role in this transformation. The recurring imagery of rain, puddles, and ultimately the breaking of the dam represents a cleansing, a return to fluidity and relationality in contrast to the rigid constructs of Western epistemology. When Lionel finds himself soaked and introspective, it is not merely an inconvenience; it marks a rebirth. His shame, embodied in the gold jacket and his job at Bursum's electronics store, begins to dissolve. What emerges is a renewed commitment to his identity, his heritage, and his potential, symbolized by his decision to return to school and pursue a degree.

The "Map" in Bursum's store, a conglomeration of televisions arranged to mimic the shape of North America, serves as a powerful visual metaphor for colonial control and cultural distortion. Its spectacle distracts and consumes, echoing the ways in which Indigenous histories have been overwritten by dominant narratives. Yet, in the hands of the four elders, even this symbol becomes a site of subversion. They hack the system, quite literally, using its own imagery to tell another story, a Native story, one that affirms identity, connection, and resistance.

In his blending of myth and realism, King rejects the "billiard ball" view of cultures as static, isolated entities. Instead, he shows that cultures are dynamic, overlapping, and constantly in conversation. This is a crucial intervention, especially in the context of Canadian multiculturalism, which too often asks immigrants and Indigenous peoples to conform to a singular cultural norm rather than honoring the multiplicity of worldviews.

Ultimately, *Green Grass, Running Water* is a testament to the resilience and adaptability of Indigenous storytelling. It asserts that narrative is not only a mode of resistance but a means of survival and resurgence. Through Coyote's chaos, Lionel's awakening, and the elders' subversive wisdom, King insists that Indigenous voices not only matter, they are essential to reimagining a more just and inclusive future.

Thomas King's *Green Grass, Running Water* examines the complex, often contradictory interplay between Native identity and the pressures of assimilation into Western, colonial structures. Through narrative, symbolism, and parody, King orchestrates a rich tapestry in which modern Indigenous people, especially Lionel and Charlie, must navigate cultural conflict, historical trauma, and personal growth. The novel critiques and reimagines traditional storytelling to create a hybrid form of resistance and survival.

One of the novel's key symbolic moments revolves around Lionel's birthday gift: a fringed leather jacket. The jacket, along with a Western film projected on Bursum's map of North America, serves as a metaphor for Lionel's internal struggle between embracing Indigenous identity or continuing to idolize colonial ideals. The film, featuring iconic white actors like John Wayne and Richard Widmark, depicts a predictable cowboy-versus-Indian narrative. Lionel, watching it, realizes how deeply he's internalized these colonial fantasies, wishing as a child to be John Wayne, not for the man himself but for what he symbolized: order, power, and righteousness.

However, this narrative is disrupted. The four old Indians, characters who are both mythic and interventionist, rewrite the script. In their version, the Indigenous characters defeat the cowboys, and John Wayne himself is shot, with bullet holes piercing the same jacket Lionel now wears. This act serves to deconstruct Lionel's reverence for colonial icons and to offer an alternative reality where Indigenous people are neither passive victims nor villains but powerful agents. The jacket, once a symbol of assimilation and denial, becomes a test, one Lionel eventually discards as suffocating. This pivotal gesture marks his symbolic return to Indigenous values and community.

King layers this narrative with mimetic rivalry, borrowing from the framework of René Girard. Lionel and Charlie, cousins and rivals, are both torn between their cultural inheritance and the expectations of Western success. They compete not only for Alberta's affection but also for identity validation in a colonial world. Charlie, now a lawyer aiding a dam project that threatens Indigenous land, and Lionel, working in Bursum's electronics store, both occupy positions that signify compromise and assimilation. Their rivalry climaxes in the dam's destruction, a moment that strips them of their colonial affiliations and forces a reconnection with their cultural roots.

Bill Bursum, owner of the electronics store, represents the pervasive influence of consumerism and Western ideology. His map of televisions arranged in the shape of North America, constantly looping Westerns, becomes a parody of imperial control and cultural flattening. Bursum believes he understands Native people because he has lived among them, failing to see how his actions and assumptions maintain systemic distances.

A critical scene that underscores this thematic return to Indigenous solidarity is the confrontation with George, a white man photographing the Sun Dance. Lionel and Eli, long passive or disconnected, physically intervene, destroying George's film. The act parallels an earlier event involving Eli's uncle, where a similar intruder succeeded in escaping. Now, the cycle has changed, Lionel actively resists colonial intrusion, signaling a shift from mimicry to agency. While Lionel is unsure what the elders have done for him, this act of resistance shows he is now acting in service of his community.

The novel also engages deeply with gender and cultural memory. Alberta, a fiercely independent academic, reflects on how marriage and colonial patriarchy threaten female autonomy. Her past relationship with Bob, a well-meaning but patronizing white man, reveals the subtle mechanisms of cultural erasure. Bob's joke about her ending up "in a teepee" if she doesn't conform to his plans reduces both her indigeneity and her womanhood to stereotypes. Alberta's choice to leave him, pursue a doctorate, and raise a child on her own terms is a radical act of resistance and reclamation.

Ada, Alberta's mother, offers another model of strength. When sacred Sun Dance items are returned damaged by border officials, Ada chooses not to dwell on loss. Instead, she begins repairing them. Her quiet resilience affirms the principle of Indigenous survival: to see clearly, act wisely, and keep moving. Her pragmatism is not submission but a refusal to let victimhood define the present or dictate the future.

At a structural level, King's storytelling style merges oral tradition with literary experimentation. The novel's cyclical, non-linear narrative mimics the rhythm of oral storytelling, where repetition, digression, and collective voice are central. Chapters open with Cherokee syllabics, and familiar myths are retold with absurd, contemporary elements, such as Ahdamn naming animals after microwaves and cheeseburgers. These juxtapositions critique Western mythologies and foreground the adaptability of Indigenous narratives. As King quips, listening to Native stories is like driving fast and veering suddenly, you either follow the turn or crash.

This narrative style problematizes beginnings and endings, favoring instead the continuity of storytelling across generations. The novel opens with a parody of Genesis, but the creation is delayed, contested, and collaboratively reshaped. "That's the wrong story," says Ishmael early on, rejecting Western canonical origins. In King's hands, creation is not a singular act of divine decree but an ongoing, dialogic process shaped by memory, humor, and human fallibility.

In the end, *Green Grass, Running Water* resists closure. Lionel's journey is not a redemption arc but a quiet repositioning, toward community, toward memory, toward continuity. Through parody, intertextuality, and narrative disruption, King crafts a novel that not only critiques colonialism but also reclaims space for Indigenous futures.

In *Green Grass, Running Water*, Thomas King uses a hybrid epigraph, beginning with the phrase "This according to The Lone Ranger" (King 1994, 8), to signal the convergence of disparate cultures and temporalities. In doing so, King playfully reimagines the canonical Gospels of Matthew, Mark, Luke, and John through the lens of iconic Western and literary figures: Lone Ranger, Ishmael, Robinson Crusoe, and Hawkeye. The incongruity of these figures, who mutate into enigmatic Indian elders adorned in bright Hawaiian shirts, gestures toward a postmodern dismantling of sacred origins and mythologies, allowing ancient and modern, East and West, cowboy and Indian, parody and canon, to coexist in a dynamic, narrative space.

This narrative collision is evident from the outset, where a creation story is humorously reimagined:

"Okay," said the Lone Ranger. "Is everybody ready?" "Hawkyee doesn't have a nice shirt," said Ishmael. "He can have one of mine," said Robinson Crusoe. "The red one?" "Yes." "The red one with the palm trees?" "Yes." (8)

King's replacement of the Gospels with four alternative narrators establishes a radical reworking of Western narrative authority. The phrase "In the beginning was the Word" becomes: "So. / In the beginning there was nothing. Just the water" (King 1994), emphasizing Indigenous cosmology and oral tradition over written doctrine.

Unlike *Medicine River*, which is more linear and protagonist-centered, *Green Grass, Running Water* is structurally diffuse. Its central character is not a single individual but the community of Blossom, a fictional, predominantly Indigenous town on the Canadian plains. Within this framework, King interweaves multiple overlapping narratives, notably the conflict surrounding Clifford Shifton's dam project. Eli, an Indigenous literature professor, returns from Toronto to his late mother's home by the river, ultimately resisting the dam's intrusion until it floods the land.

This flood, while destructive, also serves a mythic and comic function. The four mysterious elders, escaped from a mental institution, serve as narrative agents of creation and recreation. They challenge Western monotheistic narratives with lines like:

"In the beginning, God created heaven..." "That's better," said Hawkeye. "Tsane:hlanv:hi." (12)

King, whose heritage includes Cherokee, threads Cherokee syllabics and Indigenous oral structures throughout the novel. The result is a playful yet poignant challenge to Western literary and religious traditions. The four old Indians, disguised as literary icons, take on roles in absurd yet telling episodes, including the destruction of the dam using symbolic floating cars (a Pinto, a Nissan, and a Karmann Ghia), evoking the ships of Columbus and underscoring the environmental and colonial consequences of white technology.

Characters like Babo Jones, Alberta Frank, Charlie Looking Bear, and Lionel Red Dog navigate worlds defined by cultural dislocation and historical myth. Alberta, a university professor, must choose between potential fathers for her child, Charlie, a lawyer, and Lionel, a television salesman. Lionel's journey is a return to his Blackfoot roots, symbolized by his decision to live in Eli's rebuilt cabin after the flood. This return completes a circular narrative of self-discovery and cultural reintegration.

Coyote, the archetypal trickster, is a constant presence in King's metafictional landscape. He muddles stories, dreams the world into being, and even declares himself GOD:

"Where did all the water come from?" says that GOD. "I'll bet you'd like a little dry land," says Coyote. "What happened to my void?" "Hmmmm," says Coyote. "Maybe I better apologize now." (37–38)

Through Coyote, King explores the destabilization of Western binaries, good and evil, order and disorder, and replaces them with Indigenous values of balance and harmony. Coyote is both a disruptor and a healer, embodying a postmodern trickster ethos that questions the very foundation of narrative truth.

The novel's feminist subtext emerges through characters like First Woman and Alberta. Unlike the divisive Eve of Genesis, King's women maintain relational harmony. First Woman shares apples with GOD, signifying communal responsibility and interconnectedness. Female characters are not antagonistic to men but seek to revise the world through shared values and mutual respect.

Storytelling itself is a central theme, its power to shape identity, recover tradition, and "fix the world." The four old Indians, like mythic figures, move through time and space, altering narratives to align with Indigenous worldviews. Their repeated efforts to retell creation stories correctly reflect the value placed on storytelling as a process, not a product. As the narrator notes:

"We are going to have to do this again. We are going to have to get it right." (107)

This insistence on retelling speaks to the novel's circularity and its commitment to cultural survival. Stories are not static; they evolve and return, carrying new meanings each time.

In the final scenes, after the dam breaks and the flood recedes, Lionel takes up residence in Eli's cabin. The four old Indians move on, seeking the next part of the world to fix. The narrative ends not with resolution but with continuation, affirming that the act of storytelling itself is sacred, continuous, and essential.

Green Grass, Running Water is thus a postmodern, postcolonial, and deeply Indigenous narrative. Through parody, intertextuality, and the trickster figure, King invites readers to question dominant cultural paradigms and embrace the multiplicity and power of Indigenous storytelling. As King reminds us, stories shape how we see each other and the world, and in doing so, they offer the potential for healing and transformation

Here's a revised version of your comprehensive analysis, shaped into a polished, cohesive piece of nonfiction prose. The language has been refined for clarity and flow, with stronger transitions and organization while maintaining your core insights:

In many Native American cultures, storytelling is not simply an art, it is a vital act of cultural continuity and healing. As Louis Owens states, "stories have serious responsibilities: [they] tell us how we are and where we come from, make us healthy and heal us, integrate fully into the world we live in and make that world habitable, force order and reality" (*Other Destinies* 94). Similarly, Hartmut Lutz emphasizes that Native oral traditions are inherently didactic: they teach, instruct, and reaffirm identity (Lutz 198–99). Storytelling, then, is a fundamental means of strengthening tribal identity, tying individuals back into the larger web of their people, their histories, and their lands.

This vision is central to Thomas King's *Green Grass, Running Water*, a novel that interweaves myth, humor, and contemporary life to critique colonial representations and reclaim Indigenous voice. Through storytelling, repetitive, layered, non-linear, King reshapes narrative structure itself to reflect Indigenous worldviews. The novel affirms that in a tribal sense, identity is not isolated or individualistic but collective, spiritual, and rooted in communal memory and land. As Vine Deloria Jr. contends, "even the possibility of conceiving an individual only in a tribal religious sense is ridiculous" (qtd. in Lutz 197). Alienation from one's culture is not simply personal, it is mental, spiritual, and physical dislocation.

This alienation is visible in Lionel Red Dog, a central figure in King's novel, who struggles with a fractured identity. Lionel does not know who he is, but he imagines who he wants to be: a cowboy hero like John Wayne (265). This desire symbolizes a broader internalized colonialism. The dominant white society, represented through cinema, education, and economic power, portrays itself as modern, victorious, and civilized, while Indigenous culture is cast as backward, marginal, and defeated. Lionel works in a video store, endlessly deferring his dreams, trapped between two worlds and unsure where he belongs.

His aunt, Norma, understands the root of the problem: Lionel has begun to think and act like a white man (7). Like his brother Eli, who left the reserve to become a professor in Toronto, Lionel has disconnected from his cultural roots. Norma insists that regaining identity requires more than sentiment, it requires action, memory, and return. When Eli eventually comes back to live in his mother's cabin, resisting the construction of a dam that threatens tribal land, he reconnects with his community and reclaims his Indigeneity. To Norma, it does not matter why he returned; it only matters that he came home. This act of return exemplifies a "search for roots", an essential process in recovering tribal identity and agency.

King structures the novel itself as a healing ceremony. Just as Navajo healing rituals retell creation stories to realign patients with social and spiritual relationships (Moulton 83), *Green Grass, Running Water* repeats and revises four creation stories throughout the text. Each version challenges Christian and colonial myths with subversive humor and Indigenous cosmology. The native figures in these stories refuse to be subordinated to biblical archetypes. Instead, they confront and parody the narratives that have historically marginalized them, Columbus, Adam and Eve, Robinson Crusoe, and the Lone Ranger.

King uses humor as both critique and survival. As Deloria Jr. explains, tribes often "unite by sharing the mood of the past," including jokes that recall historical trauma and resistance (147). Coyote, the trickster, is central to this process. Mischievous, disruptive, and clever, Coyote embodies a storytelling tradition that is fluid, contradictory, and often irreverent. His interactions with the narrator continually destabilize any single, authoritative version of events. This dialogic structure mimics oral storytelling, where the audience is not passive but involved, shaping, challenging, and interpreting meaning.

Coyote's interruptions reflect a larger thematic concern: the clash between oral and literate cultures. Western religious and literary traditions often rely on fixed texts, immutable, hierarchical, exclusionary. Indigenous traditions, by contrast, emphasize voice, memory, and shared experience. In one of the novel's most telling scenes, the narrator tries to recount a creation story only to be interrupted repeatedly by Coyote, who insists on inserting biblical tropes: the golden calf, the pillar of salt. "Forget the book," says the narrator. "We've got a story to tell and here's how it goes" (291). In this moment, King suggests that reclaiming story means reclaiming voice, not just content but method, medium, and worldview.

Lionel's transformation culminates at the Sun Dance, a traditional ceremony that serves as a symbolic and spiritual return. There, he takes a stand for his culture by destroying photographs taken by George Morningstar, which attempted to commodify and appropriate a sacred event (422–28). This act is not merely rebellious, it is restorative. Lionel, once passive and directionless, now chooses to rebuild his grandmother's cabin and considers living there, marking a full-circle return to community and identity (464).

The four Elder tricksters, Hawkeye, Ishmael, Robinson Crusoe, and the Lone Ranger, play a pivotal role in this transformation. They are not mere comic figures; they are spiritual agents who blur the boundaries between history and myth, reality and imagination. As Marta Dvorak writes, they "have been wandering since creation trying to fix the world," representing a fusion of narrative traditions that resist simple categorization (27). Their journey mirrors Lionel's: wandering, questioning, and finally, returning.

Ultimately, *Green Grass, Running Water* enacts a

literary ceremony of renewal. It is a novel without a single protagonist, its true subject is the community of Blossom, the land it inhabits, and the stories it tells. King's critique of colonial narratives is not just thematic; it is structural. Through layered intertextuality, hybrid storytelling, and relentless humor, King dismantles the imposed authority of Christian and Western mythologies. In their place, he offers a vision of Indigenous resurgence, messy, magical, and deeply rooted in collective memory.

As King himself has argued, Indigenous literature must work against "the well-defined and entrenched images and assumptions that, over the years, were built by non-Indians, authenticated by history and literature, and sanctified by the popular mind" (qtd. in Davidson 6). *Green Grass, Running Water* is a powerful act of reimagining, offering not just resistance but a new path forward. It reminds us that stories, like communities, can be broken, but they can also be retold, reclaimed, and reborn.

Thomas King is a writer whose works confront the marginalization of Native Americans and seek to abolish long-standing stereotypes perpetuated by settler-colonial narratives. In his novel *Green Grass, Running Water*, King dismantles the imagined constructs of indigeneity shaped by the white gaze and replaces them with multifaceted, self-determined Indigenous identities. One such stereotype is encapsulated in George Morningstar, Latisha's white husband, who dons a suede jacket as a symbol of his imagined connection to Indigenous history. His belief that such an object grants him access to "authentic" Native experience epitomizes the colonial tendency to appropriate and mythologize Native culture. Latisha's cool retort, "I guess you have to know which is which", exposes the tension between fabricated and lived history, drawing attention to the settler's inability to differentiate myth from reality.

The jacket becomes a metonym for the "imaginary Indian," a figment of colonial fantasy shaped by romanticized misrepresentations. As King reveals, the Native is often rendered in white consciousness as an abstraction, detached from lived realities and molded by external projections. This simulation, as Baudrillard might argue, erases the referent and replaces it with a fetishized image. Yet through characters like Latisha and Eli Stands Alone, King illustrates a movement toward alternative representations grounded in Native perspectives.

Eli's refusal to allow a dam project to destroy his familial home reflects a powerful assertion of agency. Once perceived through the lens of typecasting, particularly by his white wife Karen who calls him her "Mystical Warrior," Eli eventually reclaims his self-worth by standing firm against development. His resistance parallels that of Elijah Harper, a real-life Cree politician who opposed the Meech Lake Accord. These symbolic victories form part of King's broader vision for a rejuvenated Indigenous consciousness.

At the heart of the novel is also a celebration of community resilience. Norma's critique of Lionel, "sometimes I think you were white", underscores the cultural alienation many Indigenous individuals face. Yet Lionel's decision to embrace his heritage and participate in the Sun Dance signals a return to cultural roots. His young niece Elizabeth, with her unrelenting cry of "Yes, I can," becomes a potent symbol of determination and hope, a spirit King suggests is vital for the reconstruction of Indigenous identity.

King employs Coyote and the four mythical elders, figures named after colonial icons such as Ishmael and Robinson Crusoe, to subvert dominant narratives. These characters traverse realms of myth and reality, reworking the Biblical story of Genesis through Indigenous oral traditions. King's playful reimagining of origin stories, in which God appears as a backwards dog, critiques the rigid patriarchy and authoritarianism embedded in Christian and colonial worldviews. Through such irreverent storytelling, King creates a narrative space where Indigenous voices can reclaim their histories.

The motif of containment, be it through the dam, prisons, or colonial discourse, serves as a central metaphor in the novel. The dam not only threatens Indigenous land but represents broader colonial attempts to restrict Indigenous agency. Similarly, Gabriel, a bureaucrat with divine pretensions, and other biblical figures function as stand-ins for colonial authority. Their absurdity and eventual failure highlight the futility of such control mechanisms.

The Dead Dog Cafe, operated by Latisha, further satirizes settler stereotypes by commodifying them. Latisha crafts an ironic performance of indigeneity tailored for tourists, selling "dog meat" and staging caricatures of Indigenous culture. This inversion not only exposes the ridiculousness of settler fantasies but also empowers Latisha by allowing her to control the narrative.

Ultimately, *Green Grass, Running Water* is an act of cultural reclamation. By infusing oral storytelling with literary narrative, King bridges traditional and contemporary forms, resisting the colonial divide between orality and literacy. As Terry Goldie suggests, the white observer historically viewed Indigenous orality as a marker of otherness. King subverts this by turning the oral tradition into a site of resistance and renewal.

Through interconnected narratives, satirical reversals, and mythological interludes, King dismantles colonial structures and offers a vision of Indigenous resurgence. In doing so, he affirms that the future of Native communities lies not in victimhood but in resilience, humor, and a relentless assertion of identity, much like Elizabeth's "Yes, I can."

In *Green Grass, Running Water*, Thomas King explores identity through what appear to be minor decisions, "mistakes," as the narrator calls them, that ultimately shape the protagonist Lionel's conflicted relationship with his cultural heritage. These mistakes offer a framework for analyzing the tension between Indigenous traditions and the pressures of assimilation.

Lionel's first mistake occurs in childhood when he falsely claims to need a tonsillectomy. This seemingly trivial lie forces his mother to take him to two types of doctors, first, traditional Blackfoot healers like Martha Old Crow and Jesse Many Guns, and then a white medical professional, Dr. Loomis. King's juxtaposition of these figures is deliberate. On the one hand, Lionel grows up in a community that respects traditional healing practices. On the other hand, his mother's decision to consult a white doctor signals openness to settler norms, hinting at the cultural divide Lionel will struggle with throughout his life. Even as a boy, he stands at a crossroads between two worlds.

Lionel's second mistake takes place during his time working for the Department of Indigenous Affairs. Sent to a conference in the U.S. to deliver a speech on behalf of his bureaucratic superior, Lionel finds himself surrounded not by policy-makers but by militant members of the American Indian Movement. Dressed in a three-piece suit among Indigenous activists in jeans and ribbon shirts, Lionel is immediately out of place. The moment underscores his alienation from the very people he ostensibly represents. Despite his discomfort, Lionel agrees to join a demonstration, only to end up, somewhat passively, in a van headed to Wounded Knee, caught between state power and Indigenous resistance. He is arrested alongside the activists, not because he shares their political ideology, but because his identity, as seen by the police, is undifferentiated from theirs.

King presents this second mistake as an emblem of Lionel's cultural dislocation. As a Canadian, a bureaucrat, and a status Indian, Lionel embodies a hybrid identity that fails to find footing in either world.

His compliance with the system contrasts sharply with the overt resistance of the AIM activists. He is neither fully assimilated nor fully committed to the cause of resistance, his presence is marked by hesitation rather than conviction.

Lionel's third mistake is his decision to stay in the town of Blossom and work for Bill Bursum's Home Entertainment Barn. This choice appears mundane, but it distances him further from his family and cultural roots. He declines to participate in preparations for his father's Sun Dance lodge, signaling a disconnect from ceremony and tradition. Though Lionel talks of returning to school, his actions speak of inertia. His life becomes a metaphor for stasis, the opposite of the transformative, communal rituals that define his father's world.

Through Lionel's missteps, King shows that identity is not a fixed category but a constantly negotiated space influenced by family, history, and personal decisions. As Marlene Goldman suggests, King's narrative resists essentialist notions of authenticity. Rather than drawing rigid lines between "real" and "inauthentic" Indians, King celebrates cultural hybridity while remaining committed to Indigenous sovereignty and traditions. This balancing act is at the core of his work, rejecting the binary logic of colonial discourse in favor of complexity and nuance.

In both *Medicine River* and *Green Grass, Running Water*, King uses interpersonal relationships to mirror broader cultural tensions. Louise's relationship with Will in *Medicine River* is emblematic of cautious, respectful coexistence. The two characters navigate their relationship slowly, embodying a model for how Indigenous and settler communities might engage with each other, not through domination, but through mutual understanding.

Children born from mixed unions serve as powerful symbols of this vision. In *Medicine River*, South Wing, fathered by a white man and embraced by a Native family, embodies hope for a more inclusive future. Similarly, in *Green Grass, Running Water*, Elizabeth represents a forward-looking assertiveness that is neither constrained by colonial memory nor detached from Indigenous heritage. Through these characters, King disrupts the rigid structures of colonial categorization. These children, products of mixed heritage, are portrayed not as marginal but as central figures who carry the potential for renewal and transformation.

By rewriting literary and cultural narratives, King refuses to let Indigenous characters be trapped in what he calls the "literary limbo" of white representations. His fiction liberates them to reclaim authorship over their own stories, cultural practices, and futures.

Nature is not just a backdrop in King's fiction; it is a central character and ideological force. He contrasts the permanence falsely promised by technology with the enduring cycles of the natural world. In *Green Grass, Running Water*, this opposition is dramatized through the construction of a dam, which threatens to disrupt not just ecosystems but cultural practices like the Sun Dance. The dam symbolizes colonial imposition and environmental exploitation, while the river stands for Indigenous continuity and resilience.

Harley tells Eli that the dam prevents the river from delivering nutrients to the cottonwood trees used in the Sun Dance lodge, illustrating how environmental degradation threatens ceremonial life. The phrase "as long as the grass is green and the waters run" becomes a bitter irony, it is no longer just a metaphor, but a broken promise. King insists that true permanence lies not in concrete and control, but in the reciprocal relationships between land, people, and ceremony.

Ultimately, King's literary project is one of reclamation, of identity, of narrative authority, and of the land itself. His nuanced, often humorous explorations of cultural hybridity, ecological harmony, and storytelling traditions reveal a vision of Indigenous life that is dynamic, resilient, and deeply rooted in both history and possibility.

❑

CHAPTER-V

Configurations of Native Cultural Identity in Truth and Bright Water

In *Truth and Bright Water*, Thomas King constructs a richly layered narrative that explores Native cultural identity through the lens of ceremonial restoration, artistic intervention, and trickster discourse. At the heart of the novel is a profound attempt to reconfigure the social and political structures imposed upon Indigenous histories, drawing attention to the enduring power of cultural storytelling, tribal memory, and ceremonial reimagination. Through characters like Monroe Swimmer and Tecumseh, King crafts a literary space where Indigenous voices reclaim agency against the backdrop of colonial erasure and commodification.

King deploys trickster discourse and historical intertextuality as tools of resistance, using narrative deception and irony to interrupt and amend the dominant stories of Indigenous tragedy and cultural extinction. The novel performs what Gerald Vizenor refers to as "mythical verism," a narrative realism that resists the anthropological gaze and replaces it with cultural tenacity and resilience. In King's world, Native experience is not a static archive but a dynamic, living reality that thrives through imagination, art, and storytelling.

This cultural reworking is embodied most powerfully in the character of Monroe Swimmer, an artist and trickster figure who returns to his community with the intention of restoring both art and ceremony. Swimmer's work, retrieving Indigenous remains from museums, restoring landscape paintings by inserting Indigenous figures, and staging fire ceremonies, serves as a symbolic and literal reclamation of space and identity. He infuses lost cultural fragments with new meaning, creating continuity between the past and the present. His ceremonial fire, held during the Indian Days Festival, becomes a transformative communal act that reasserts cultural presence in the face of commercial spectacle and tourist consumption.

King critiques the commodification of Native culture through the portrayal of the Indian Days Festival, where traditions are packaged for tourist consumption. German tourists flock to buy "authentic" Indian artifacts and food, enacting a shallow engagement with culture that reduces it to novelty. Swimmer's work acts as an antidote to this trend, offering ceremonial acts that are not for sale but for community healing. His giveaway ceremony emphasizes not the material exchange but the gathering itself, a space where people come together to remember, celebrate, and renew their ties to the land and to each other.

The motif of bones, literal and symbolic, runs throughout the novel, representing both colonial desecration and the potential for cultural reclamation. Swimmer's mission to recover Indigenous skulls from museum drawers and return them to the land reclaims ancestral dignity and interrupts the imperial project of turning Native bodies into anthropological artifacts. By placing the bones back into their rightful context, Swimmer restores their cultural significance and resists the narrative of Indigenous disappearance. As he says, "This is the centre of the universe… Where else would I bring them? Where else would they want to be?"

The skull Tecumseh finds not only halts his storytelling but also exposes the settler project's attempt to fossilize Native identity. Yet, Swimmer's interventions disrupt these closures. He brings the dead back into the present, allowing them to speak through ritual and art. His role as trickster magician, making buffaloes reappear as sculptures in the coulees, "restoring" them to the land, underscores the novel's aesthetic and political aims. Through trickster magic, King challenges the dichotomy between reality and fantasy, advocating for a hybrid narrative space that reflects the complexity of Indigenous identity.

King's use of humor, subversion, and irony, hallmarks of the trickster figure, enables multiple readings of the text. Swimmer is not merely comic relief; he is the catalyst for reimagining the community's relationship with its past and with itself. His character embodies the androgynous, shape-shifting liberator described by Vizenor, capable of navigating and disrupting colonial structures through performance, inversion, and art.

In contrast, the tragic figure of Lum represents the damaging effects of cultural disconnection and identity fragmentation. Abused and isolated, Lum cuts his hair and paints his body in the stylized image of a movie Indian, a desperate attempt to belong. His transformation is both an act of mourning and a reflection of cultural disfigurement. His death becomes a somber warning about the consequences of unresolved identity and cultural alienation. King illustrates how the pressure of navigating between Indigenous heritage and dominant white society can result in tragic outcomes, especially when ceremonial frameworks for healing are absent.

Tecumseh, guided by Monroe, begins to understand that identity is not purely individual but intricately tied to communal memory and cultural narrative. The restoration of ceremony, whether traditional or reimagined, emerges as a necessary process for personal and collective healing. King's vision, however, is not simplistically optimistic. He acknowledges that returning to one's culture is not always redemptive; many characters remain caught in liminal spaces, unable to reconcile their inherited traditions with the demands of the present. Yet, within these struggles lies the potential for transformation, particularly through the reactivation of cultural imagination.

Ultimately, *Truth and Bright Water* is an act of literary resistance, one that refuses closure and champions the ceremonial as a living, adaptive force. Through Monroe Swimmer's art and trickster interventions, King advocates for a cultural continuity that honors the past while embracing new forms of expression. The novel does not propose a single solution to Indigenous identity in a colonized world, but it insists on the importance of storytelling, ceremony, and collective memory in shaping futures that are both rooted and dynamic.

Certainly. Here's a polished nonfiction prose version shaped from the ideas and analysis in your text. It reads like an academic or reflective critical essay:

In *Truth and Bright Water*, Thomas King critiques the institutional authority of museums and the complicity of scholars in the ongoing colonial project of collecting and preserving Native remains. Through Monroe Swimmer, a flamboyant, enigmatic artist and former museum restorer, King dramatizes the act of repatriation, presenting it as both a spiritual ceremony and a political intervention. Museums, in King's novel, are not temples of preservation but mausoleums for cultures rendered inert by academic categorization and state-sponsored curation. In contrast, Monroe's work is restorative and alive, functioning as a redemptive practice of reburial and remembrance. He recovers Native bones from the museum vaults and returns them to the Shield River, transforming the river into a sacred and natural sepulcher.

This act of return connects water, bones, and

memory. The novel's imagery reinforces this symbolic network: "In the distance, clouds are on the move... they look like long, slender bones... they float over the horizon as if they were being carried along the river" (49). The river, fluid, liminal, and flowing between the U.S. and Canada, functions not just as a geographical boundary but as a metaphor for cultural transmission, for the in-between space where life, memory, and spirit converge.

The Shield River, as a motif, is central to the novel's exploration of memory and identity. It serves as a border, a burial ground, and a symbolic space of continuity between the living and the dead, tradition and transformation. The abandoned bridge between Bright Water and Truth, with its minimal crossings, either a long detour or a precarious cable ferry, echoes the difficulty of moving between imposed political categories and Native ways of knowing.

King's critique extends to cultural commodification. The "Indian Days" festival becomes a battleground for meaning, where traditional practices are reenacted not for ceremony, but for tourism. Tecumseh, the young narrator, is disillusioned with his community's complicity in staging buffalo hunts as tourist spectacles. The event's authenticity is undercut by its commercial frame. As Robert Berkhofer and Stuart Hall have argued, the recreation of Indigenous traditions for non-Native audiences reduces them to performance and parody. These staged moments obscure the complex histories they represent, risking the transformation of sacred cultural practice into consumable spectacle.

King's narrative resists such flattening by embedding the subversive potential of art. Monroe Swimmer is not merely a painter but a trickster figure who reclaims imperial landscapes. His vision is restorative: "Under his costume as a crazy-artist, there is a man... who is really aware of the great political, historical and economic issues" that underlie Indigenous dispossession. Art, in Monroe's hands, is not decorative but reparative. He reclaims rail-scarred meadows with iron-wire buffalo sculptures, reversing imperial logic through creative resistance. These buffalos, silent, metallic, and haunting, do not exist for show; they are rhetorical agents, symbolic presences that unsettle colonial narratives. They are "magic," as Monroe insists, not realism. Their stillness invokes lost herds, ancestral power, and the spiritual continuity of land and memory.

Alongside Monroe's art, King explores the tension between oral and written traditions. He collapses binaries, oral/written, mother/father, art/nature, within a trickster framework that privileges ambiguity and layered meaning. Greek myth, often overlooked in King's criticism, plays a crucial role. These stories, like Indigenous oral narratives, were originally passed down through speech and later codified in writing and performance. They too deal with generational trauma, family conflict, and the ethics of inheritance. King's invocation of Greek myth aligns with his larger project: to deconstruct Eurocentric literary paradigms by folding them into Native storytelling.

This interplay is vividly realized in the skull

motif. Tecumseh and Lum discover a skull, polished and placed with intention. "The skull is the problem," Tecumseh muses, foreshadowing the narrative's meditation on history, death, and identity (69). The skull evokes Hamlet and the theatricality of loss; it is both a symbol of personal grief and a critique of anthropological practices that reduce Native remains to museum exhibits. Lum, who hoists the skull "like a wand or a flag," becomes an Indigenous Hamlet, haunted by familial trauma and the weight of a history that refuses to stay buried.

Lum's arc is central to the novel's structure of disappearance and return. His final race across the bridge becomes a symbolic vanishing act, a gesture toward transcendence that doubles as a surrender to despair. The community's silence about his abuse, his unresolved grief for his mother, and his thwarted desire to participate in a meaningful tradition, all culminate in his tragic disappearance into the mist. His death is not just a personal loss, but a communal wound, a reminder that not all recoveries are possible.

Yet even in this loss, the novel offers gestures of hope and survival. Monroe's mentorship of Tecumseh marks a turning point. Through art and music, Western tools, yes, but recontextualized within Indigenous frameworks, Tecumseh begins to heal. The gifted piano lessons, not inherently Native, become part of a broader therapeutic repertoire, underscoring the adaptability of Native culture rather than its erasure. Helen, his mother, grounds him in Native mythology, while Monroe opens a space for creativity, resistance, and imagination.

Indian Days, for all its commercial trappings, also represents continuity. As Brien Osborne notes, it functions as a memorial ritual, a time of eating, storytelling, and gathering. It is both modern and ancient, commodified and sacred, fractured and whole. These paradoxes lie at the heart of *Truth and Bright Water*, which insists that culture is not static but dynamic, not pure but hybrid. Art, memory, and ceremony remain sites of survival and regeneration.

In King's vision, realism will only take us so far. The return of the buffalo, whether made of flesh or iron, requires magic. And magic, in this context, is not illusion but transformation: the ability to see differently, to remember deeply, and to reimagine what has been lost.

Certainly! Here's your text restructured into a cohesive nonfiction prose analysis of *Truth and Bright Water* by Thomas King, emphasizing Monroe Swimmer's aesthetic interventions, symbolic representations like the quilt and the buffalo, and the broader colonial critique embedded in King's narrative style:

In *Truth and Bright Water*, Thomas King reimagines Indigenous identity through a complex interplay of art, restoration, and colonial satire. At the heart of this narrative is Monroe Swimmer, a character whose eccentric artistry both critiques and subverts colonial representations of Indigenous absence. His central project, the illusionary disappearance of a church and the restoration of buffalo to the land, enacts a form of aesthetic decolonization, blurring the line between artifice and spiritual renewal.

The iron calf, or buffalo sculpture, stands as a potent symbol of this process. These sculptures are not mimetic; they are outlines in iron, shaped by the mind's eye rather than the imaginative potential of realism. "Accuracy is important," Monroe asserts, "but absolute historical truth is a dangerous Euro-western fantasy." His statement targets the colonial impulse to freeze Indigenous cultures in ethnographic stasis, turning living traditions into picturesque ruins. Where colonial discourse offers sympathy and documentation, Monroe offers imagination and transformation. The buffalo, functioning simultaneously as regional icon, pan-Indian emblem, decorative relic, and cultural artifact, becomes a locus of Indigenous resilience.

Yet, Monroe's methods are fraught with irony. By making the church disappear, he seems to symbolically reclaim the land. But this act, a visual trick, inverts the colonial trope of the "empty land" by recreating it through Indigenous artifice. The church, though unseen, still exists, "I did not lose the church... I just lost track of it", and Tecumseh, the young narrator, must navigate this illusion carefully, extending his hand like a blind man to avoid colliding with its ghostly presence. King satirizes the very idea of replacement, mocking simplistic reversals of power: "maybe he is going to tear the damn thing down and put up a tipi."

This irony extends to Monroe's buffalo. Though three hundred and sixty sculptures are erected across the landscape, each a unique silhouette, they are simultaneously real and not real. Some of them even appear to come to life, while the actual buffalo from Indian Days mysteriously vanish and reappear near the sculptures. The narrator often can't distinguish between the living and the iron: "when they stop moving and stand still, they look like rocks." The trope of fossilization speaks to the precariousness of restoration, how the animate can become inert, how memory solidifies into myth.

Elvin, Tecumseh's father, provides a counterpoint to Monroe's romanticism. For Elvin, the buffalo are not noble symbols but reminders of stubbornness and failure: "Buffalo are stupid... Just like the Indians." His cynical retelling of history, that the buffalo simply "took off and never came back", rejects the tragic narrative of extermination, casting instead a story of abandonment and missed opportunity. For Elvin, even history is suspect.

Meanwhile, Monroe's restoration efforts, though well-intentioned, verge on constructing a theme park version of the past. The community's participation in Indian Days, driven by tourism and spectacle, reduces tradition to performance. King challenges readers to question whether such acts are reclaiming culture or merely replicating colonial frameworks under different aesthetics. Monroe's bonfire, in which he empties the church and distributes its contents to the community, is cathartic but also ambiguous, healing through spectacle.

Helen, Tecumseh's mother, offers another

mode of resistance. Through her quilt, a tapestry of geometric forms, found objects, and symbolic motifs, she weaves a private narrative of loss, resilience, and transformation. Unlike the uniform, machine-stitched Mennonite quilts, Helen's creation is eclectic and deeply personal. In it, one finds the communities of Truth and Bright Water, stitched together by the river Shield, rendered in fabric, feathers, fishhooks, and thread.

Helen's quilt is not merely decorative, it is a living text. As Deborah Weagel suggests, "a quilt is a text... that speaks its maker's desires and beliefs, hopes and fears." Through its evolving patterns and unusual inclusions, Helen's quilt documents the dissolution of her marriage, her frustrations, and her survival. It is both autobiography and political commentary. Tecumseh, who does not seek to interpret the quilt directly, nonetheless becomes its narrator, preserving his mother's visual language within the larger narrative of the novel.

The title itself, *Truth and Bright Water*, signifies a divided landscape, one town American, the other Canadian, separated by the river Shield. The river begins "in ice," emphasizing stasis and cold beginnings, but also symbolizing liminality and potential. The half-built bridge across it, intended to connect the two communities, instead symbolizes disconnection, unfinished reconciliation, both literal and figurative. The river's name, "Shield," is suggestive too: a boundary, a form of protection, or a surface upon which stories are painted. For Monroe, the land by the river is "the centre of the universe", a sacred site where memory, art, and resistance converge.

Ultimately, *Truth and Bright Water* presents a Native identity that is elusive, layered, and often paradoxical. Restoration, whether through sculpture, illusion, or quilt, is not about returning to an authentic, verifiable past, but about reimagining relationships in the present. King's satirical tone and pan-Native approach question the validity of both colonial and Indigenous essentialisms. In this novel, the path toward healing lies not in rigid fidelity to tradition, but in the creative stitching together of fractured histories into new, meaningful forms.

Certainly! Here's a refined and structured non-fictional prose analysis based on the points you've raised about Helen's quilt, the concept of border crossings, and other significant themes from *Truth and Bright Water*:

In *Truth and Bright Water*, Thomas King intricately weaves political, social, and cultural layers through the character of Helen, whose personal journey is expressed through the metaphorical and material fabric of her quilt. Helen's quilt-making is more than a personal catharsis or an act of artistic expression; it is an autobiographical text that reflects her evolving relationship with her Indigenous identity and political consciousness.

Helen's quilt is not merely a representation of her troubled marriage or individual struggles. Rather, it becomes a politically charged artifact, signaling her commitment to expressing her Native origins. Her quilt, a traditional American patchwork style, incorporates a bold use of colors and patterns reminiscent of Native art, offering a subversive commentary on colonial representations of Indigenous culture. Through the quilt, Helen learns to reclaim her identity and assert her voice in ways that transcend the traditionally private and domestic realm of women's work. In *Patchwork Quilts: Finding Women's Social and Political History in Modern Material Culture*, Marie Battiste notes that quilts have historically provided women with a silent form of political commentary when more overt expressions of dissent were deemed inappropriate. For Helen, the quilt is an act of self-empowerment, a way of asserting her political identity while reflecting on the history and struggles of her people.

Suzanne Rintoul further expands on this, suggesting that King links the oral traditions of Native culture with femininity and maternity, while simultaneously drawing attention to the trivialization of women's communication in colonial discourse. Helen's quilt becomes a tool of resistance in the same way Helen of Troy's voice was reduced to a catalyst for war; in King's novel, Helen's concerns are dismissed by her husband, Elvin, who blames her for the problems in their relationship. By quilting, Helen speaks where she would otherwise be silenced, reclaiming the agency that Elvin tries to strip away. The quilt thus functions as a space where Helen's private struggles meet the broader, collective narrative of Indigenous survival and adaptation.

As her confidence grows, Helen's political

assertiveness extends beyond the quilt and into the public sphere. She plays the role of the Queen in a satirical theater production that critiques the federal government's treatment of Indigenous peoples. This play, described as a "political satire about the federal government and the Indians," positions Helen as a figure who, through both her art and her involvement in community theater, begins to publicly challenge the structures that have long oppressed her people. In doing so, Helen not only reclaims her identity as a Native woman but also redefines her role in her community and her family.

The symbolic weight of the quilt extends beyond personal identity, offering a broader commentary on survival and cultural preservation. As Helen uses the quilt to weave her own personal history, she simultaneously reinterprets the very medium that colonial powers introduced to her people. Nancy Parezo's assertion that "Indian people have survived because we have been very flexible, we adapt" captures the essence of Helen's artistic endeavor. The quilt, a craft introduced by European settlers, becomes a canvas through which Helen adapts and reinterprets her Indigenous heritage. Her quilt thus functions as a space of both cultural survival and resistance, where the values of her ancestors are preserved and reimagined within the context of her personal and communal experiences.

Paula Gunn Allen's comparison of the patchwork quilt to traditional tribal narrative underscores the significance of Helen's work. Like the oral traditions of her people, the quilt is a medium for storytelling, yet it is uniquely individual and female. Allen writes that the quilt is "the best material example" of the "plot and process of traditional tribal narrative," where different elements are sewn together to create a cohesive whole. Similarly, Helen's quilt represents the fragmentation and reconstitution of her life, each patch a symbol of her struggle, survival, and reinvention. Through it, she gives voice to her history, her pain, and her resilience.

The metaphor of the quilt extends into the novel's broader thematic concerns of division and connection. Helen's quilt not only represents her individual survival but also reflects the disjointed state of the community itself. Tecumseh's observations of the quilt and his difficulty in identifying the figures depicted within it reveal the broader existential crisis of living on the margins of both Canadian and American society. Tecumseh is caught between two worlds, his father's world and his mother's, and the quilt becomes a symbol of his own search for belonging. His confusion about the identities represented in the quilt mirrors his larger struggle with identity, as he attempts to reconcile his position as a Native person caught between the two sides of the US/Canada border.

This theme of border crossings is central to *Truth and Bright Water*, as it reflects not only the literal division between the two countries but also the figurative divides that characterize Native life in North America. King explores the complexities of identity through his characters' movement across national borders, challenging the artificiality of these boundaries. The border between Canada and the United States is "a line of someone else's imagination," a concept that echoes throughout King's work, as his characters confront the limitations imposed by colonial borders. The border is not just a physical boundary but a symbolic one, a space where Native people are continually defined and redefined by external forces.

The novel's title, *Truth and Bright Water*, itself references the treaty language that promised Indigenous lands as long as "the rivers flow," emphasizing the symbolic importance of water in Native culture. Water, like the border, serves as both a literal and metaphorical crossing point, linking different worlds while simultaneously separating them. The unfinished bridge that spans the river in the novel is a powerful symbol of the ongoing struggle to bridge the gap between the Indigenous and settler communities, a gap that remains unhealed despite attempts at reconciliation.

In King's narrative, the trickster figure plays a pivotal role in destabilizing the cultural assumptions of both Native and non-Native communities. Monroe Swimmer, an artist in the novel, embodies this trickster energy as he reinterprets colonial symbols like the buffalo and the church, using art to both expose and resist the forces that seek to erase Indigenous identity. His project of restoring the buffalo through iron sculptures is an act of reclaiming history, an effort to reinsert Indigenous presence into landscapes from which they have been erased. This subversive art project, alongside the satire of the border and the manipulation of public spaces, critiques both the colonial past and the ongoing colonial practices that continue to marginalize Indigenous peoples.

Ultimately, *Truth and Bright Water* presents a nuanced exploration of the complexities of identity, survival, and resistance within a colonial context. Helen's quilt serves as both a personal and political artifact, weaving together her history, her heritage, and her struggle for recognition. Through her, King underscores the importance of reclaiming Native identity not just through cultural expression, but through political and communal participation. The narrative itself becomes a powerful commentary on the ways in which colonialism continues to shape the lives of Indigenous peoples, while also offering pathways for decolonization through art, satire, and community building.

❑

CHAPTER-VI

The Territory Ahead for Native Studies and the Works of Thomas King

Native Literature, as a field of study, increasingly focuses on the presence and importance of trickster figures and the ways in which they reflect the interplay between Native and colonial identities. While the academic landscape now includes a broader focus on Native Literature, particularly through the lens of Canadian literature studies, a significant challenge remains in the dissemination and understanding of Native works. This challenge is rooted in a dominant preoccupation with writers and their texts, which often overlooks the cultural and identity concerns embedded within these works. Penny Petrone's *First People, First Voices* (1983) has been instrumental in emphasizing the necessity of studying culture and identity within Native literature, a sentiment that continues to resonate today.

Thomas King, in his "Introduction" to *All My Relations*, asserts that Native writers employ trickster figures to engage deeply with cultural concerns, specifically the need for balance and harmony. King observes that Native characters are often portrayed as resourceful, vibrant, and resilient, unlike their counterparts in colonial and mainstream literature, who are typically depicted as inferior or dying. Native characters, like traditional tricksters, face hardships, being tricked, beaten, robbed, and ridiculed, but they persist, survive, and, at times, thrive. These characters resist the colonial definitions imposed upon them, offering a counter-narrative to the erasure and dehumanization prevalent in non-Native representations.

This idea of the trickster is not merely a literary trope but a critical tool for reimagining colonial narratives and colonial power structures. As Gerald Vizenor and Carlton Smith argue, the trickster is a "liberative" figure, whose disruptive actions challenge established categories of understanding and perception. The trickster is mimetic, performing a range of functions, from affirming traditional values to challenging colonial power. This dynamic is essential in understanding Native literature, as it unveils the fluid, changeable nature of identity, which contrasts with the static, fixed conceptions of self often imposed by colonial forces.

Native identity, as expressed through the trickster figure, is inherently fluid. King emphasizes the importance of community in defining the self, contrasting Native conceptions of identity with the Western, oppositional understanding of the individual versus society. In Native culture, identity is shaped by integration into one's social grouping, kin, clan, or band. This understanding reflects an anti-colonial stance, as it disrupts the colonial desire for a fixed, singular identity that overlooks diversity and differences within colonized peoples.

In *Green Grass, Running Water*, King takes this fluidity of identity further by embodying it in the characters' experiences and in their resistance to colonial representations. For example, Lionel, a procrastinator trapped between his desires and societal expectations, represents a contemporary Native figure who rejects colonial limitations in favor of self-definition and cultural renewal. The text also explores the intersection of Native and Biblical narratives, showing how the trickster, Coyote, challenges conventional religious and cultural interpretations. This blurring of boundaries between sacred figures and colonial representations of the divine critiques both the construction of the "Native" and the assumptions embedded in Western theological narratives.

The process of identity construction in King's works also involves an interrogation of the self in relation to the community and the land. Margaret Harry Wong's reflection on Native autobiography aligns with this, as she argues that self-narration and self-representation are essential to the process of identity formation. King's novels, particularly *Medicine River* and *Green Grass, Running Water*, underscore the significance of the community in shaping individual identity, showing that while Native characters often struggle with isolation and loss, they ultimately find a sense of belonging and purpose through their connections to their cultural heritage.

Moreover, King's novels challenge colonial representations through humor and wit. King uses humor as a weapon against oppression, as it exposes the absurdity of colonial ideologies and stereotypes. This comedic approach is not merely for entertainment but is deeply political, subverting colonial authority by undermining the seriousness of racist attitudes. As Margaret Atwood notes, King's humor is a tool of resistance, allowing him to critique colonialism without resorting to anger or confrontation.

King's novels also explore the tension between individual desires and communal responsibilities, often focusing on Native characters who must navigate the complexities of modern life while remaining connected to their cultural roots. The characters in King's works, such as Lionel in *Green Grass, Running Water*, are deeply affected by the colonial legacy but find ways to reclaim and redefine their identity through resistance and renewal. King's portrayal of Native spirituality, both sacred and flawed, acknowledges the imperfections within Native culture while also affirming its vitality and relevance in contemporary life.

Through his works, King reveals the ongoing impact of colonialism on Native peoples, particularly the ways in which colonial representations distort and marginalize Native experiences. At the same time, he provides a space for Native voices to assert their agency and resist these colonial constructions. By destabilizing and reimagining colonial narratives, King's works invite readers to reconsider their assumptions about identity, culture, and history, ultimately contributing to a broader understanding of Native experiences in North America.

The notion of boundaries and borders is central to King's protest against colonial structures. His use of humor, myth, and oral tradition allows him to resist the colonial imposition of fixed identities and to offer a vision of Native culture that is dynamic, multifaceted, and capable of transcending binary constructions of the colonizer and the colonized. King's works, then, are not just protests against colonialism but also powerful tools for reshaping our understanding of identity, culture, and history. Through the use of trickster figures, humor, and narrative innovation, King offers a compelling vision of Native resistance and cultural survival in a contemporary world.

In *Green Grass, Running Water*, Thomas King intricately weaves together themes of tradition and modernity through the characters and their interactions with both the physical and cultural landscapes of their lives. Central to this exploration is the depiction of the Sun Dance, a sacred and powerful event for the Blackfoot peoples, lasting eight days. This festival, a time for prayers, dancing, singing, and offering, takes place in the circle of tepees and lodges, serving as a spiritual anchor for the community. Within this setting, the character of Eli Stands Alone embodies the complex interplay between the traditional and modern, standing as a bridge between two worlds. His connection to the Sun Dance is both symbolic and deeply rooted in personal history; he recalls his mother's lodge, always placed on the eastern side of the circle, a reminder of his cultural heritage and familial ties to the land. Eli's character defies easy categorization, serving as an anti-stereotype, one who leverages his experiences in the "white world" to assert his identity as both modern and Native. In his dialogue with his sister Norma, who clings to more traditional views, Eli asserts, "Nothing wrong with getting away from the reserve. We have been here thousands of years. That's my profession. Being Indian is not a profession." Through this, King emphasizes the tension between maintaining cultural identity and adapting to contemporary realities.

In the narrative, the Indian Days festival becomes a moment of active cultural participation, showcasing characters such as Fenton Bull Runner and his wife Maureen, who make dream catchers, and Edna Baton, who runs a fry bread stand. These everyday activities, dream catchers, beadwork, and fry bread, serve as expressions of cultural continuity, connecting the present generation with their ancestors in both tangible and symbolic ways. King also highlights how the commercialization of Native culture, as seen through the selling of cassettes of old-time pow wow songs by Jimmy Hunt and his family, presents a complicated relationship between cultural preservation and economic necessity. Yet, Monroe Swimmer, an artist and key figure in the narrative, offers a more symbolic contribution to the festival. He relinquishes his wealth, giving away items that reflect both his life and the lives of those in the community. Monroe's gifts, a woman's painting, a Navajo rug, and a set of Japanese armor, are deeply personal yet transcend their materiality, embodying King's theme of cooperative sharing. These acts of generosity reflect Native cultural values that prioritize community and collective well-being over individual ownership.

Monroe's character is crucial in King's larger project of reclamation. He serves as a mouthpiece for King's cultural stories, using his art to restore Native presence in spaces where they have been erased or misrepresented, particularly in Western art and history. Monroe's return of Native artifacts from museums around the world is a powerful gesture of reparation and cultural reclamation, a move that echoes King's broader critique of colonialism and its impact on Indigenous peoples. By painting Indians back into artworks where they were once excluded, Monroe reasserts their rightful place in both history and art.

King's narrative structure, marked by its fragmentation, disjointed dialogues, and multiple points of view, further reflects the oral traditions of Native storytelling. This non-linear, digressive mode mimics the flow of oral narratives, which do not follow a clear trajectory or adhere to Western conventions of causality and sequence. The disjointedness of King's writing, as described by Gzowski, mirrors the very instability and fluidity of Native oral traditions. King's novels, therefore, not only critique colonialism and the appropriation of Native stories but also offer a new form of storytelling that resists the rigid constraints of Western literary forms. King's use of various signifiers, objects, characters, and voices, creates a tapestry of meaning that does not rely on linear progression, emphasizing the richness and complexity of Native cultural perspectives.

Through his exploration of the impact of settler media on Native peoples, King interrogates how colonial hybridization has shaped Native identities. Critics like Goldman have analyzed how King reworks the colonial legacy of orality and writing, showing that these two forms of expression are not opposing forces but rather intertwined practices that can both challenge and reshape Western forms of knowledge and representation. King's ambivalence toward the Western reliance on written narratives is clear; he critiques the Eurocentric notion of progress, which seeks to dominate and control both human and non-human life. This worldview, which elevates technology and industry above all else, stands in stark contrast to the Native recognition of the impermanence of human existence and the interconnectedness of all life forms. King's work resists this Eurocentric worldview, advocating instead for a more inclusive and holistic conception of existence, one that values the cultural practices, histories, and lives of Indigenous peoples.

In this way, King's *Green Grass, Running Water* is not merely a narrative about individual characters but a larger commentary on the relationship between Native peoples and the forces of colonialism, both past and present. Through his complex narrative techniques, characters like Eli and Monroe, and his focus on cultural reclamation, King offers a profound critique of settler-colonial narratives while also celebrating the resilience and vitality of Native cultures. The novel invites readers to reconsider the ways in which stories, both oral and written, can be used as tools of resistance, healing, and cultural preservation.

❑

Works Cited

- Adamson, Joni, Mei Mei Evans, and Rachel Stein, editors. *The Environmental Justice Reader: Politics, Poetics, and Pedagogy*. University of Arizona Press, 2002.
- Allen, Paula Gunn. *The Sacred Hoop: Recovering the Feminine in American Indian Traditions*. Beacon Press, 1986.
- Ashcroft, Bill, Gareth Griffiths, and Helen Tiffin. *The Empire Writes Back: Theory and Practice in Post-Colonial Literatures*. Routledge, 1989.
- Bhabha, Homi K. *The Location of Culture*. Routledge, 1994.
- Brady, Miranda J. "Mediating Indigenous Voice: Indigenous Actors, Canadian National Media, and the Imagined Audience." *Canadian Journal of Communication*, vol. 37, no. 3, 2012, pp. 335–354.
- Brazeau, Karen. "The Trickster in Contemporary Native American Literature." *Studies in American Indian Literatures*, vol. 3, no. 2, 1991, pp. 33–43.
- Chamberlin, J. Edward. *If This Is Your Land, Where Are Your Stories? Finding Common Ground*. Vintage Canada, 2003.
- Deloria, Vine Jr. *God Is Red: A Native View of Religion*. Fulcrum Publishing, 1973.
- Fee, Margery, and Jane Flick. "Coyote Pedagogy:

Knowing Where the Borders Are in Thomas King's *Green Grass, Running Water.*" *Canadian Literature*, no. 161–162, 1999, pp. 131–139.
- Fitz, Earl E. *Modernism and the Question of Translation: A Study of Latin American Literature.* University of Alabama Press, 2018.
- Fitzgerald, Stephanie. "Intimate Geographies: Reclaiming Land and Stories in Thomas King's *The Truth About Stories.*" *American Indian Culture and Research Journal*, vol. 34, no. 1, 2010, pp. 75–92.
- Foucault, Michel. *The Archaeology of Knowledge.* Translated by A.M. Sheridan Smith, Pantheon Books, 1972.
- Hulan, Renée. *Northern Experience and the Myths of Canadian Culture.* McGill-Queen's University Press, 2002.
- Hutcheon, Linda. *A Theory of Parody: The Teachings of Twentieth-Century Art Forms.* Methuen, 1985.
- King, Thomas. *The Truth About Stories: A Native Narrative.* House of Anansi, 2003.
- King, Thomas. *Green Grass, Running Water.* HarperPerennial Canada, 1993.
-
- King, Thomas. *Medicine River.* Penguin Canada, 1989.
- King, Thomas. *Truth and Bright Water.* HarperFlamingo Canada, 1999.
- King, Thomas. "Godzilla vs. Post-Colonial." *World Literature Written in English*, vol. 30, no. 2, 1990, pp. 10–16.
- King, Thomas. "You're Not the Indian I Had in

Mind." *The Massey Lectures*, CBC Radio, 2003. Transcript available at House of Anansi.
- Krupat, Arnold. *Ethnocriticism: Ethnography, History, Literature*. University of California Press, 1992.
- Krupat, Arnold. *The Voice in the Margin: Native American Literature and the Canon*. University of California Press, 1989.
- LaRocque, Emma. *When the Other Is Me: Native Resistance Discourse, 1850–1990*. University of Manitoba Press, 2010.
- McLeod, John. *Beginning Postcolonialism*. 2nd ed., Manchester University Press, 2010.
- Momaday, N. Scott. *The Way to Rainy Mountain*. University of New Mexico Press, 1969.
- Moss, Laura. "Thomas King's *Green Grass, Running Water*: Border Crossings and Cultural Hybridity." *Canadian Literature*, no. 161–162, 1999, pp. 114–132.
- Owens, Louis. *Other Destinies: Understanding the American Indian Novel*. University of Oklahoma Press, 1992.
- Ridington, Robin. "Coyote's Cannon: Sharing Knowledge and the Language of Literature." *Canadian Literature*, no. 161–162, 1999, pp. 145–154.
- Silko, Leslie Marmon. *Storyteller*. Penguin Books, 1981.
- Smith, Linda Tuhiwai. *Decolonizing Methodologies: Research and Indigenous Peoples*. 2nd ed., Zed Books, 2012.

- Vizenor, Gerald. *Manifest Manners: Narratives on Postindian Survivance*. University of Nebraska Press, 1999.
- Womack, Craig S. *Red on Red: Native American Literary Separatism*. University of Minnesota Press, 1999.
- Warren, Jean. "Trickster Discourse in Thomas King's *Green Grass, Running Water*." *Studies in Canadian Literature / Études en littérature canadienne*, vol. 20, no. 2, 1995, pp. 82–102.
- Fee, Margery. "Who Can Write as Other? Ethical, Political, and Practical Issues in Aboriginal Representations." *The Canadian Review of American Studies*, vol. 27, no. 2, 1997, pp. 227–247.
- Goldie, Terry. *Fear and Temptation: The Image of the Indigene in Canadian, Australian and New Zealand Literatures*. McGill-Queen's University Press, 1989.
- Hutcheon, Linda. *The Politics of Postmodernism*. 2nd ed., Routledge, 2002.
- Heble, Ajay, et al., editors. *New Contexts of Canadian Criticism*. Broadview Press, 1997.
- Heble, Ajay. "The Semiotics of Identity: Teaching Thomas King's *Green Grass, Running Water*." *Canadian Literature*, no. 161–162, 1999, pp. 44–62.
- Hoy, Helen. *How Should I Read These? Native Women Writers in Canada*. University of Toronto Press, 2001.
- Justice, Daniel Heath. *Our Fire Survives the Storm: A Cherokee Literary History*. University of Minnesota Press, 2006.

Black Eagle Books

www.blackeaglebooks.org
info@blackeaglebooks.org

Black Eagle Books, an independent publisher, was founded as a nonprofit organization in April, 2019. It is our mission to connect and engage the Indian diaspora and the world at large with the best of works of world literature published on a collaborative platform, with special emphasis on foregrounding Contemporary Classics and New Writing.

www.ingramcontent.com/pod-product-compliance
Lightning Source LLC
Chambersburg PA
CBHW060617080526
44585CB00013B/870